Library of Presi[dential Rhetoric]

Martin J. Medhurst, General Editor

WRITING JFK

Writing JFK

Presidential Rhetoric and the Press
in the Bay of Pigs Crisis

THOMAS W. BENSON

Texas A&M University Press : College Station

The paper used in this book meets the minimum requirements
of the American National Standard for Permanence
of Paper for Printed Library Materials, Z39.48-1984.
Binding materials have been chosen for durability.

Frontispiece: John F. Kennedy and Theodore Sorensen,
White House South Lawn, March 12, 1963. Courtesy John F. Kennedy Library.

An earlier version of chapter 2 was published in the Working Paper Series of the Joan
Shorenstein Center on the Press, Politics, and Public Policy at the John F. Kennedy School of
Government, Harvard University, which granted permission to publish this material here.

Library of Congress Cataloging-in-Publication Data

Benson, Thomas W.
Writing JFK : presidential rhetoric and the press in the Bay of Pigs
crisis / Thomas W. Benson.—1st ed.
p. cm. — (Library of presidential rhetoric)
Includes bibliographic references (p.   ) and index
ISBN 1-58544-276-3 (alk. paper) — ISBN 1-58544-281-x (pbk. : alk. paper)
1. Kennedy, John F. (John Fitzgerald), 1917–1963—Relations with
journalists.   2. Cuba—History—Invasion, 1961.   3. Rhetoric—Political
aspects—United States—History—20th century.   4. Press and politics—
United States—History—20th century.   5. Presidents—
United States—Language—History—20th century.
I. Title.   II. Series.
E842.1.B46   2003
972.9106'4—dc21   2003009576

For my wife,
Margaret Sandelin Benson,
and our daughters,
Daisy Benson and Sarah Benson

Contents

Acknowledgments

I am grateful to many colleagues and associates who offered support and advice as this book was in preparation.

This book was begun in the spring of 1999 when I was a research fellow at the Joan Shorenstein Center on the Press, Politics, and Public Policy at the John F. Kennedy School of Government, Harvard University. The support of the fellowship made possible an intense period of research at the Harvard Libraries and at the nearby John F. Kennedy Presidential Library. I am grateful to the then director of the Shorenstein Center, Marvin Kalb, to Professor Thomas Patterson, and Edith Holway, Marion Just, Pippa Norris, Nancy Palmer, and Richard Parker of the Center for creating an ideal climate for focused research and ongoing conversations. To the other Shorenstein fellows of my cohort, Michael Goldfarb, William Hammond, Xiguang Li, and Alina Pippidi-Mungiu, and to Wolfgang Donsbach, who was Lombard visiting professor at the Shorenstein Center in spring, 1999, my thanks for support and good fellowship. Thanks to Kathleen E. Kendall, who was a Shorenstein fellow in spring, 1997, for encouraging me to consider spending a semester at the Center. I am grateful to Senator Alan Simpson, who was director of the Institute of Politics during my fellowship semester at Harvard, and to the staff and fellows of the Institute, for many courtesies and opportunities for fruitful discussion. Thanks to the Nieman Foundation and the Nieman Fellows for hospitality and conversation, and to the staff of the Harvard University Libraries.

For sharing their candid and thoughtful recollections of working in the Kennedy White House, I am grateful to Theodore C. Sorensen, who was special counsel to the president, and to Carl Kaysen, David W. Skinner Professor of Political Economy Emeritus in the Program in Science, Technology, and Society at the Massachusetts Institute of Technology, who served as the Deputy Special Assistant for National Security Affairs. For interviews on presidential speechwriting in the Kennedy White House I am grateful to David Bell, Archibald Cox, and Arthur M. Schlesinger, Jr.

My colleagues and students at the Pennsylvania State University make it a happy and productive place to work. I am grateful to Dennis Gouran and Michael Hecht, who have served as heads of the Department of Speech Communication while this book was in preparation, and to Susan Welch, dean of the College of the Liberal Arts; all have been generous in going beyond the routine levels of support for my work. I am grateful to my colleagues in rhetoric at Penn State, especially to the late Richard B. Gregg and to Stephen Browne, Herman Cohen, J. Michael Hogan, and Christopher Johnstone. The endowment of the Edwin Erle Sparks Professorship of Rhetoric at the Pennsylvania State University, originally funded by private donations and a matching grant from the National Endowment for the Humanities, has made much of the research possible. Graduate and undergraduate students at Penn State are a continuing inspiration.

The photograph of John F. Kennedy and his speechwriter and counsel Theodore Sorensen was taken on the White House South Lawn on March 12, 1963, by photographer Robert Knudsen of the Office of Naval Aide to the President. The photograph is part of the collection of the National Archives and Records Administration (control number NLK-WHP-KN-KN27169), and is used here courtesy of the John F. Kennedy Library.

Much of the research for this book was conducted at the John F. Kennedy Library in Boston, Massachusetts, during the spring of 1999 and on several other visits. I offer my thanks to the staff of the Library for their assistance in locating materials used in this book. The presidential libraries of the United States are a national treasure, informing the ongoing national self-criticism that makes democracy real.

An earlier version of chapter 2 was originally presented at a research seminar at the Shorenstein Center, and was later published in the Working Paper Series of the Center. I am grateful to Harvard University for permission to publish this material.

My thanks to Martin J. Medhurst, my former student and for many years my friend, coauthor, colleague-at-a-distance, and the editor of the Texas A&M University Press series in which this volume appears.

To my wife Margaret, and to our daughters Daisy and Sarah, to whom this book is dedicated, my love and thanks.

John F. Kennedy's Address before the American Society of Newspaper Editors, April 20, 1961

Mr. Catledge, members of the American Society of Newspaper Editors, ladies and gentlemen:

The President of a great democracy such as ours, and the editors of great newspapers such as yours, owe a common obligation to the people: an obligation to present the facts, to present them with candor, and to present them in perspective. It is with that obligation in mind that I have decided in the last 24 hours to discuss briefly at this time the recent events in Cuba.

On that unhappy island, as in so many other arenas of the contest for freedom, the news has grown worse instead of better. I have emphasized before that this was a struggle of Cuban patriots against a Cuban dictator. While we could not be expected to hide our sympathies, we made it repeatedly clear that the armed forces of this country would not intervene in any way.

Any unilateral American intervention, in the absence of an external attack upon ourselves or an ally, would have been contrary to our traditions and to our international obligations. But let the record show that our restraint is not inexhaustible. Should it ever appear that the inter-American doctrine of non-interference merely conceals or excuses a policy of nonaction—if the nations of this Hemisphere should fail to meet their commitments against outside Communist penetration—then I want it clearly understood that this Government will not hesitate in meeting its primary obligations which are to the security of our Nation!

Should that time ever come, we do not intend to be lectured on "intervention" by those whose character was stamped for all time on the bloody streets of Budapest! Nor would we expect or accept the same outcome which this small band of gallant Cuban refugees must have known that they were chancing, determined as they were against heavy odds to pursue their courageous attempts to regain their Island's freedom.

But Cuba is not an island unto itself; and our concern is not ended by mere expressions of nonintervention or regret. This is not the first time in either ancient or recent history that a small band of freedom fighters has engaged the armor of totalitarianism.

It is not the first time that Communist tanks have rolled over gallant men and women fighting to redeem the independence of their homeland. Nor is it by any means the final episode in the eternal struggle of liberty against tyranny, anywhere on the face of the globe, including Cuba itself.

Mr. Castro has said that these were mercenaries. According to press reports, the final message to be relayed from the refugee forces on the beach came from the rebel commander when asked if he wished to be evacuated. His answer was: "I will never leave this country." That is not the reply of a mercenary. He has gone now to join in the mountains countless other guerrilla fighters, who are equally determined that the dedication of those who gave their lives shall not be forgotten, and that Cuba must not be abandoned to the Communists. And we do not intend to abandon it either!

The Cuban people have not yet spoken their final piece. And I have no doubt that they and their Revolutionary Council, led by Dr. Cardona—and members of the families of the Revolutionary Council, I am informed by the Doctor yesterday, are involved themselves in the Islands—will continue to speak up for a free and independent Cuba.

Meanwhile we will not accept Mr. Castro's attempts to blame this nation for the hatred which his onetime supporters now regard his repression. But there are from this sobering episode useful lessons for us all to learn. Some may be still obscure, and await further information. Some are clear today.

First, it is clear that the forces of communism are not to be under-estimated, in Cuba or anywhere else in the world. The advantages of a police state—its use of mass terror and arrests to prevent the spread of free dissent—cannot be overlooked by those who expect the fall of every fanatic tyrant. If the self-discipline of the free cannot match the iron discipline of the mailed fist—in economic, political, scientific and all the other kinds of struggles as well as the military—then the peril to freedom will continue to rise.

Secondly, it is clear that this Nation, in concert with all the free nations of this hemisphere, must take an ever closer and more realistic look at the menace of external Communist intervention and domination in Cuba. The American people are not complacent about Iron Curtain tanks and planes less than 90 miles from their shore. But a nation of Cuba's size is less a threat to our survival than it is a base for subverting the survival of other free nations throughout the hemisphere. It is not primarily our interest or our security but theirs which is now, today, in the greater peril. It is for their sake as well as our own that we must show our will.

The evidence is clear—and the hour is late. We and our Latin friends will have to face the fact that we cannot postpone any longer the real issue of survival of freedom in this hemisphere itself. On that issue, unlike perhaps some others, there can be no middle ground. Together we must build a hemisphere where freedom can flourish; and where any free nation under outside attack of any kind can be assured that all of our resources stand ready to respond to any request for assistance.

Third, and finally, it is clearer than ever that we face a relentless struggle in every corner of the globe that goes far beyond the clash of armies or even nuclear armaments. The armies are there, and in large number. The nuclear armaments are there. But they serve primarily as the shield behind which subversion, infiltration, and a host of other tactics steadily advance, picking off vulnerable areas one by one in situations which do not permit our own armed intervention.

Power is the hallmark of this offensive—power and discipline and deceit. The legitimate discontent of yearning people is exploited. The legitimate trappings of self-determination are employed. But once in power, all talk of discontent is repressed, all self-determination disappears, and the promise of a revolution of hope is betrayed, as in Cuba, into a reign of terror. Those who on instruction staged automatic "riots" in the streets of free nations over the efforts of a small group of young Cubans to regain their freedom should recall the long roll call of refugees who cannot now go back—to Hungary, to North Korea, to North Viet-Nam, to East Germany, or to Poland, or to any of the other lands from which a steady stream of refugees pours forth, in eloquent testimony to the cruel oppression now holding sway in their homeland.

We dare not fail to see the insidious nature of this new and deeper struggle. We dare not fail to grasp the new concepts, the new tools, the new sense of urgency we will need to combat it—whether in Cuba or South Viet-Nam. And we dare not fail to realize that this struggle is taking place every day, without fanfare, in thousands of villages and markets—day and night—and in classrooms all over the globe.

The message of Cuba, of Laos, of the rising din of Communist voices in Asia and Latin America—these messages are all the same. The complacent, the self-indulgent, the soft societies are about to be swept away with the debris of history. Only the strong, only the industrious, only the determined, only the courageous, only the visionary who determine the real nature of our struggle can possibly survive.

No greater task faces this country or this administration. No other challenge is more deserving of our every effort and energy. Too long we have fixed our eyes on traditional military needs, on armies prepared to cross borders, on missiles poised for flight. Now it should be clear that this is no longer enough—that our security may be lost piece by piece, country by country, without the firing of a single missile or the crossing of a single border.

We intend to profit from this lesson. We intend to reexamine and reorient our forces of all kinds—our tactics and our institutions here in this community. We intend to intensify our efforts for a struggle in many ways more difficult than war, where disappointment will often accompany us.

For I am convinced that we in this country and in the free world possess the necessary resource, and the skill, and the added strength that comes from a belief in the freedom of man. And I am equally convinced that history will record the fact that this bitter struggle reached its climax in the late 1950's and the early 1960's. Let me then make clear as the President of the United States that I am determined upon our system's survival and success, regardless of the cost and regardless of the peril!

Note: The president spoke at the Statler Hilton Hotel in Washington. His opening words "Mr. Catledge" referred to Turner Catledge, president of the American Society of Newspaper Editors, and managing editor of the *New York Times*. Later in his remarks the president referred to Dr. José Miró Cardona, president of the Cuban Revolutionary Council.

The text of the address, including the note, is taken from *The Public Papers of the President* (1961).

WRITING JFK

CHAPTER 1

Writing JFK

Shortly after midnight on April 17, 1961, a band of Cuban exiles, under the direction of the United States government, attacked Cuba at and near the Bay of Pigs. The invasion, which had been rumored in the press for weeks, was a disaster. Within two days most of the invading force was killed or captured, as the United States struggled to deny, then defend, its actions. John F. Kennedy, who had been president for less than three months, asked himself, "How could I have been so stupid as to let them proceed?" Others were asking the same question. As the events in Cuba were unfolding, Kennedy went on with his earlier commitments to appear in public. Among these commitments were speeches to the American Society of Newspaper Editors, on April 20, and to the American Newspaper Publishers Association, on April 27. Those two speeches, and the story of their creation and reception in the midst of an unfolding crisis of leadership, are the subject of this book.

This book is a case study in the construction of John F. Kennedy's presidential leadership through public rhetoric; about the authorship of that rhetoric; and about the mediation of that rhetoric through the press. I explore the relation of press, public rhetoric, and presidential speechwriting as interacting forces that contributed to the writing of the presidency of JFK. Kennedy on occasion spoke directly to the press; all of his speeches were reported through the press, which shaped and filtered the nation's sense of what Kennedy had said; several of his most important speeches were written partly with direct or indirect contributions from the press. In a sense, Kennedy's speeches and the press as an influence before and after those speeches weave themselves inseparably into one larger rhetorical text. But if the textual elements are in many ways inseparable, the separate threads are discernible, and when examined in the retrospective magnifying glass of rhetorical inquiry have much to tell us about the processes of contemporary government.

John Kennedy's assassination in November, 1963, seemed at the time, and has ever seemed in retrospect, a tragic turning point in the American experience, coloring as it did our subsequent national derangement in Vietnam and Watergate, and in the political murders of Malcolm X; Michael Schwerner; James Chaney; Andrew Goodman; Medgar Evers; Martin Luther King, Jr.; Robert Kennedy; and others. The assassination of President Kennedy also gave rise to a counter-current, however—the myth of Camelot and the urgency of completing the Kennedy legacy through the great domestic programs of the Lyndon Johnson administration, chiefly in civil rights and the Great Society programs in medical care, education, and social welfare.

The power of the presidency to make myth and change history, revealed in the events following November, 1963, had a history in somewhat less apocalyptic developments. The Kennedy presidency was a time of accomplishment and crisis. The two speeches studied in this volume are not his most eloquent or celebrated, though they are among the most revealing. A reader looking for the most eloquent Kennedy speeches might turn to the inaugural address, and to the transformative speeches of two days in June of 1963, when he turned sharply toward a more peaceful tone in relations with the Soviet Union and when he took upon himself the claim that civil rights had reached a stage of "moral crisis" for the nation. Only the president could have enacted the rhetorical gestures of the American University commencement address of June 10, 1963, and the civil rights address of June 11, 1963. Although others might have made the arguments offered in those speeches, only the president could have said the precise words, and only the president could have enacted the performances embodied in those speeches. And yet President Kennedy was not the sole author of his speeches, and most of his speeches became known to his audiences through the contexts, interpretations, and mediation of the press. How that process worked—how John F. Kennedy's utterances came to be made and understood—is the subject of this investigation. The greatest of Kennedy's speeches depended on the lessons, the practices, and the talents that had been exercised week after week over a period of many years, and that are revealed vividly in the speeches he made during the Bay of Pigs crisis.

The methods I use in this study are largely historical and critical, but I do hope that something like a grounded theory of one aspect of presidential rhetoric may emerge. Rhetorical analysis involves a double historical task of trying to reconstruct what happened in some complex set of events and what seemed to have been happening to those who were involved in those events at the time. We will never, looking back, be able to reconstruct a perfectly complete or impartial understanding of a rhetorical episode, but the attempt to make such a reconstruction can help us to recapture something of the particular moment and to understand more fully the experience of living in a rhetorical world. Presidential speeches are created and spoken under conditions where outcomes are, by definition, uncertain, and where every participant is likely to have a somewhat different set of purposes, understandings, and impressions. And yet presidential speaking—like most rhetorical interaction—partly has the effect of bringing some coherence to the multiplicity of points of view. How that coherence is achieved—or not—and what is remembered or forgotten, noticed or ignored, in its achievement has historical and rhetorical importance.

At the conceptual level, this book addresses the relations among presidential speechwriting, presidential speechmaking, and press coverage of presidential rhetoric. Presidential speeches influence political discourse, policy, and public opinion. In an important sense, they may be said to constitute policy not only by influencing through argument but also by enacting through performance. The structures of speechwriting influence both speech texts and policy formation. The press mediates and in some ways formulates presidential rhetoric. We need to know more about how these processes work. In this exploration of press, speechwriting, and presidential rhetoric, I use two case studies of speeches early in the Kennedy administration to understand the two-way processes by which presidential rhetoric is addressed *to* the press, *through* the press to the public, using materials written in public and behind the scenes *by* the press, and *over* the heads of the press to the public; at the same time, these cases illustrate how both the public and the press contribute to presidential rhetoric by providing material to the speechwriting process itself. Hence, the processes of rhetorical influence run not only from but also to the president in a complex cycle with many possible variations.

Presidential speechmaking has long been of interest to scholars of rhetoric, of the presidency, and of the relations of press and politics. I draw on these somewhat disparate traditions in this study of the speeches of John F. Kennedy.

In his book *The Rhetorical Presidency*, Jeffrey Tulis argues that Theodore Roosevelt and Woodrow Wilson introduced a new feature of the presidency. Both men not only spoke more frequently than their nineteenth-century predecessors, but also they developed a practice of speaking over the heads of Congress to the people. This practice, writes Tulis, is a historical development not anticipated by the Constitution and, though it has become commonplace, it is not inevitable. The rhetorical presidency may tend to hinder rather than advance deliberative democracy, since a president has no Constitutional equal and tends not to commit to public rhetoric until he has come to the point of advocating a particular program of action.[1]

In *Spin Control*, John Anthony Maltese traces the history of the White House Office of Communications from its invention by President Richard Nixon as a means of allowing the president to speak over the heads of the press, and especially of the national press, to the people and to local and regional media, thus avoiding the critical mediation of specialized political journalists. In adopting the practice of holding regular, live, televised news conferences, over considerable protest from newspaper journalists, John F. Kennedy can be understood in retrospect as having advanced the means by which presidents can speak over the heads of the press.

Every scholar of Kennedy and the press is indebted to Montague Kern, Patricia W. Levering, and Ralph B. Levering, whose 1983 book *The Kennedy Crises: The Press, the Presidency, and Foreign Policy* investigates press-presidency interaction in four Kennedy foreign policy crises—Laos and Berlin in 1961, Cuba in 1962, and Vietnam in 1963, working "toward an understanding of the conditions under which the press can apply pressure on a president and, conversely, the influence that he can have on press coverage."[2] In this present volume I work in a slightly different direction from that of Kern, Levering, and Levering, concentrating on Kennedy's speechmaking in two case studies that combine foreign and domestic issues and that, implicitly and explicitly, concern the press itself as the subject under discussion. I hope that this difference in focus, and the availability of additional documentary and interview sources, will amplify our understanding of John F. Kennedy's complex rhetorical leadership and its relationship with the press. Kern, Levering, and Levering begin their book by describing how Kennedy speechwriter Theodore Sorensen solicited ideas for an October, 1961, speech from Joseph Alsop, Walter Lippmann, and other journalists. "What is especially significant in this episode is not that they gave long and thoughtful replies, parts of which were incorporated into the speech, but rather that the president was putting these prominent columnists in a position where it would be more difficult to criticize his policies."[3] Although it is true that Kennedy and Sorensen gained influence over journalists and academics by this tactic, and had done so at least since the 1960 presidential campaign, as had other presidents and candidates before them, it seems to me that it is also important to pay serious attention to what presidents say and how they come to say it. Presidential speeches have an enduring importance as the discourse of democracy. In presidential rhetoric, quality matters as much as success, which itself can be immediate or long-term, direct or indirect. Often, the side effects of a presidential speech are as important as any direct effects, especially as those side effects accumulate over time. Furthermore, success is judged not only from the perspective of the administration, but also from the perspectives of other agents, including the press and the public. Hence, in this account, I examine closely the texts of two presidential speeches; the processes of speech composition; and the complex ways in which press and public interacted with the speeches as acts and as texts. Kern, Levering, and Levering reported that they were attempting to "represent two academic disciplines, political science and history, each with its own methodology and approach to knowledge," one interested in the theoretical and methodological, the other in chronology and particularity.[4] Their book makes an enduring contribution; it is hoped that the rhetorical perspective of my book adds something to the conversation.

A number of rhetorical scholars have made notable contributions to the study of John F. Kennedy's speeches. Their work is cited in context in the course of the following chapters. Among the works published most recently are Steven R. Goldzwig and George N. Dionisopoulos, *"In a Perilous Hour": The Public Address of John F. Kennedy;* Vito N. Silvestri, *Becoming JFK: A Profile in Communication;* Kimber Charles Pearce, *Rostow, Kennedy, and the Rhetoric of Foreign Aid;* and Garth E. Pauley, *The Modern Presidency and Civil Rights: Rhetoric on Race from Roosevelt to Nixon.*[5]

The development of the presidency as a rhetorical office has led a number of scholars to comment on how the office has changed. Theodore Lowi, in *The Personal President: Power Invested, Promise Unfulfilled,* describes a situation in which a president can win an election by a large margin, but in which he does not transfer his strength to his party. The result is a personal presidency, even what he calls a "plebiscitary republic." Lowi attributes the modern growth of presidential power to Franklin Roosevelt, placing considerable emphasis on the personalization of presidential power under JFK, particularly under the influence of Richard Neustadt's *Presidential Power.* Presidents have to promise more than they can deliver, argues Lowi, and even when they do deliver, this just raises expectations; all this leads to attempts to manipulate the appearance of success, largely through news management and rhetoric. Lowi's analysis, if correct, would explain how, as the presidency during and after Roosevelt sought new powers, it was necessary for the president to speak more and more frequently, leading, in turn, to the employment of speechwriters, and the changes naturally brought about by the institutionalization of that function. The speeches thus produced would, of course, be designed in part to advance the president's policies, but they would also, and importantly, be used to deploy the sense of the president's enormous political and personal potency. Lowi finds the process that was begun under FDR advanced to completion with John F. Kennedy:

> Completion of the task of redefining the presidency as necessary for the government and for national democracy followed the 1958 congressional elections and the 1960 presidential election. The most important of the authors at that time was Richard Neustadt, whose book *Presidential Power* became the bible of the Kennedy administration and, to say the least, the leading text on the subject among political scientists and journalists. Neustadt's book is based on the thoroughly realistic assumptions that the American national government would not work unless the presidency was effective, and that no president could be effective unless he constantly concerned himself with how each decision he made advanced his power over the administration, the Washington community, Congress, and the people. Since the president's only real power was "the power to persuade," he had to manipulate each of his constituencies in order to use each for the manipulation of the other.[6]

In this book, I argue:

- that the rise of the *ghostwritten presidency* is one feature of the expanding role and the personalization of the presidency in the modern era,
- that the presidential *speeches* and the press relations of John F. Kennedy contributed to a personalization of the presidency, elaborating a depiction of Kennedy, his audience, and other rhetorical agents, and

- that the *press* of the Kennedy period developed a complex rhetoric of subjectivity, attribution, and personification that is a clear foundation for the press practices of the 1990s that attracted the complaints of so many journalists, academic critics, and politicians.

This book is an account of rhetorical agency and its depiction in two speeches by John F. Kennedy—of the way they came to be written, the context in which they were enacted, and the ways in which the press interpreted them. The two speeches occur in April 1961, in the immediate aftermath of the failed Cuban invasion at the Bay of Pigs, when Kennedy spoke to the American Society of Newspaper Editors (ASNE) on April 20, and then to the American Newspaper Publishers Association (ANPA) on April 27.

The two speeches display the implicit and characteristic collaboration of Kennedy with his speechwriters and the press to create a depiction of Kennedy as a political and moral agent. In the ASNE speech, Kennedy is a president in trouble after the failed invasion of Cuba; the press largely mirrors Kennedy's self-depiction as learning from his mistakes and as requiring loyal support in a time of danger. In the ANPA speech, Kennedy appealed to the press to be responsible to issues of national security. The speech was generally regarded as a failed attempt at news management and threatened to sour the portrayal of Kennedy that had emerged just a week before.

Together, these two speeches reveal various dimensions of the complex relations among the press, the speechwriter, and the president as they collaborate to construct the public story of the presidency. The press and the president collaborate to construct a frame that emphasizes the president's subjective point of view, a narrative device that predisposes the reader toward empathy, but that can turn against a president when the press presumes to reveal disreputable motives on the part of a president. The press is a client of the information supplied by the presidency, and in the case of the ANPA speech the press was the public audience for a direct appeal for restraint in the interests of national security. Indirect restraints were constantly practiced; direct restraints were rejected.

John F. Kennedy's speeches to the American Society of Newspaper Editors and the American Newspaper Publishers Association are competent and compelling rhetorical performances, though they do not rank in eloquence or perhaps in wisdom with his very greatest speeches. Kennedy's inaugural address and his speeches of June, 1963—first in a commencement address at American University on foreign policy (June 10, 1963) and the next day in declaring that civil rights was a moral crisis (June 11, 1963)—are greater speeches, and they, too reveal interesting features of the interactions among presidential speech making, speech writing, and the press. Indeed, in a conversation with Theodore Sorensen at Harvard University in the spring of 1999, Mr. Sorensen winced when I said that I was planning to write about the ASNE and ANPA speeches of April, 1961, and nodded approvingly when I said I was also planning in a later project to write about the American University and civil rights speeches of June, 1963. And yet the ASNE and ANPA speeches do have a claim on our attention in their own right and for what they can reveal of the processes of presidential rhetoric. These two speeches of April, 1961, reveal a pattern that unfolded in the rest of the Kennedy presidency and that has been elaborated in the decades since. The enormous power of the presidency to compel press restraint and to command the powers of publicity are inseparable, disguising a complex collaboration in the construction of the rhetorical text of the presidency by the president, his speechwriters, and the press.

CHAPTER 2

The Responsible Officer
of the Government

The Bay of Pigs and the Speech to the
American Society of Newspaper Editors

In April, 1961, President John F. Kennedy was approaching the important symbolic marker of 100 days into the presidency, evoking press assessments of his success. Kennedy was scheduled to give speeches to the American Society of Newspaper Editors (ASNE) on April 20, and the American Newspaper Publishers Association (ANPA) on April 27. In the week before the ASNE speech, Cuban exiles invaded the Bay of Pigs. The anti-Castro forces were quickly defeated; most were captured; some were executed. The event was a serious embarrassment for Kennedy and his administration and brought forth intense scrutiny of his performance. The Cuban invasion also prompted a change in plans for what Kennedy would say to ASNE and ANPA.

President Kennedy addressed the American Society of Newspaper Editors at the Statler Hilton Hotel in Washington, D.C., on April 20, 1961. As the theoretical context for this analysis, I draw on two lines of inquiry that I hope to bring into a closer relation to each other. The first is the study of "agency" and "identity" within the rhetorical tradition. The second line of inquiry is the rapidly expanding body of research on the relations among press, politics, and public policy that has been the focus of the Joan Shorenstein Center on the Press, Politics, and Public Policy at the John F. Kennedy School of Government at Harvard University. Every use of rhetoric immediately raises issues of motive and intention, and at the same time makes those issues nearly impossible to resolve authoritatively. As a practical matter, a persuasive discourse is not merely a collection of arguments or inducements to act in our own best interest, but depends fundamentally on projecting a convincing depiction of the speaker's character, competence, and intentions—what Aristotle called *ethos*. We cannot, of course, know another's intentions infallibly, but in our relations with other humans we cannot act without some assessment of those intentions.

Following Aristotle, rhetorical theorists have for centuries studied ethos, or character, as one of the primary sources of persuasion. George Kennedy translates the famous passage from Aristotle's *Rhetoric* as claiming that, "[There is persuasion] through character whenever the speech is spoken in such a way as to make the speaker worthy of credence; . . . character is almost, so to speak, the controlling factor in persuasion."[1]

Twentieth-century rhetorical studies have extended the study of ethos and have related it to the study of how the speaker depicts not only his or her own character and identity but also those of the listener and other agents in the situation.[2] Kenneth Burke has been the most influential and comprehensive rhetorical theorist in the twentieth century to address common-sense and philosophical structures of motivation and to link those understandings to a theory of persuasion as identification. In *A Grammar of Motives*, Burke demonstrates that both the history of philosophy and our everyday understandings of human interaction are guided by assumptions about motivation. We ask of any action, says Burke, what happened, who did it, how, with what purpose, when and where. In his *A Rhetoric of Motives*, Burke establishes a theory of persuasion based on identification. These two analytical perspectives combine to form the structure of Burke's notion of dramatism as the ground of human symbolic action and its interpretation. Burke's theories have been absorbed into rhetorical studies and are often implicit in this analysis of the production, performance, and reception of John F. Kennedy's rhetoric.

In his 1994 book *Out of Order,* Thomas E. Patterson writes that reporters covering presidential candidates generally give them more bad press than good. "Reporters have a variety of bad-news messages, but none more prevalent than the suggestion that the candidates cannot be trusted. When candidates speak out on the issues, the press scrutinizes their statements for an ulterior motive. Most bad-news stories criticize candidates for shifting their positions, waffling on tough issues, posturing, or pandering to whichever group they are addressing."[3]

Patterson argues that "the rules of reporting changed with Vietnam and Watergate, when the deceptions perpetrated by the Johnson and Nixon administrations convinced reporters that they had let the nation down by taking political leaders at their word."[4]

And so, says Patterson, reporters developed a schema of distrust, typically assuming that a president has ulterior motives. This schema is reinforced by a press that, according to Patterson, is increasingly lazy— and it might be added lacking in resources and time, with decreasing news cycles—and so instead of actually comparing a president's statement with the facts of the matter, they "found a substitute for careful investigation. They began to use a president's opponents as the basis for undermining his claims."[5]

Patterson argues that, "As late as the 1960s, the news was a forum for the candidates' ideas. Looking back at the election coverage of the 1960s, one is struck by the straightforward reporting of the candidates' arguments.... The candidates' statements had significance in their own right—an arrangement that no longer holds." Patterson then develops an extended comparison between coverage of John F. Kennedy in the 1960 campaign and of Bill Clinton in the 1992 campaign. In 1992, in contrast to 1960, writes Patterson, "the message [was] refracted through the press's game schema."[6] Many observers claim that in reporting the investigation and impeachment of President Clinton, the press went still further in its pursuit of the private life of a president and its reports on his thoughts and feelings. Deborah Mathis, the White House correspondent for Gannett News Service, argues that the press routinely engaged in "hearsay journalism" in reporting the President's thoughts and feelings.[7]

Patterson makes a persuasive, even a compelling case that something happened to press coverage of political rhetoric after Watergate and Vietnam, but there is some evidence that the roots of these developments may be seen in press coverage of earlier presidents.

In this chapter I explore from another direction, and from an earlier time, the ways in which the press covers political rhetoric and the ways in which "motive" forms part of the narrative of political speechmaking. The administration of John F. Kennedy reveals an emerging configuration of three elements that contributed to Kennedy's rhetoric and its reception:

- The *production* of the speeches, which typically involved the initial drafting of a Kennedy speech by Theodore Sorensen or another speechwriter.
- The *texts* of the speeches, especially as they imply authorship, intention, and agency.
- The *press accounts* of the speeches, both in their interpretation of the argument of the speech and in their depiction of the president and his motives, intentions, and inner states.

My investigation is not intended as a test of Patterson's claims for the superiority of press accounts of political argument in the Kennedy era, nor do I claim that Patterson is mistaken in tracing the dominance of the "ulterior motive" schema to the Watergate and Vietnam experiences. The "game schema" described by Patterson, in which "ulterior motives" are ascribed to a presidential candidate, are so effective partly because they appeal to our common sense. My hope is to apply critical methods to understand the structures of common sense that appear to govern rhetorics of agency and identity, and to apply historical methods to the discovery of how those common-sense structures were produced and disseminated.

In the early 1960s, political journalism was actively re-examining its practices, and showing signs of chafing under old constraints. The inventor of "direct cinema," Robert Drew, with his colleagues Ricky Leacock and Donn Pennebaker, went "behind the scenes" of the Democratic primary in Wisconsin to film Hubert Humphrey and John Kennedy as they spoke to small groups, shook hands on the street, met with their advisors, and drove from one small town to another.[8] Theodore White transformed political reporting in *The Making of the President, 1960*, which initiated a long series of behind-the-scenes reports on American politics.[9]

During the Kennedy presidency, we have some explicit evidence that the mainstream press was restless with the rules of political reporting. In 1960, Joseph Alsop worried that younger political reporters were not doing their homework about history and policy, and were too willing to rely on government press agents, though he did acknowledge that on occasion reporters needed to be prodded by government. In a lecture at the University of Minnesota, Alsop told the story of George Marshall's speech at Harvard, announcing the Marshall Plan: "There was no special announcement . . . that Marshall was going to Harvard to receive a degree and make a key speech. . . . Consequently, Marshall's announcement of his Marshall Plan, which, if anything has changed history in the postwar period, did change history, very nearly went completely unnoticed. Officials had to call up and point out that the speech was of outstanding importance before it received adequate attention in the national press."[10]

Like Patterson in the 1990s, Alsop in 1960 worries that reporters are getting lazy, but instead of making the reporters of 1960 overly suspicious, he argues, it is likely to make them too tame. He warns aspiring political reporters, "Don't be too humble. . . . I don't think it's possible to be both a serious, self-respecting newspaperman and a spaniel."[11] Alsop urges reporters to be adversarial, but sees the solution coming from a return to former standards, in resistance to practices originated in creeping government press-agentry.

Other press critics argued that a robust adversary press could come only from the introduction of new standards and techniques. John Fischer, the editor of *Harper's Magazine,* speaking at the University of Minnesota in 1962, urged his colleagues to be suspicious of the constraints of objectivity. Fischer said that when he covered the U.S. Senate for the Associated Press, "I . . . felt myself increasingly hampered by the conventions of objectivity that were standard then—and still are to a large extent—with all newspaper organizations, especially with the press associations. I was constantly reporting what somebody said, even though I knew that it was untrue, misleading, or self-serving. There was no way within the canons of press association work that I could indicate that a senator or witness before a Senate committee was telling a damn lie."[12]

Fischer cites John Hersey's book *Hiroshima* (1946; 1989) and H. L. Mencken's reporting on political conventions as instances of first-person reporting that produced not only good writing but also superior insight, and which might form the basis for new experiments that ventured beyond the constraints of objectivity.

Both Alsop and Fischer appear to be taking a fairly long-term perspective on the interaction of press and politics. During the Kennedy presidency, there were several more immediate developments that prompted reflections about politics and the press. Among the developments often cited as crucial are Kennedy's introduction of live, televised press conferences; administration charges that the press violated national security interests at the time of the Cuban invasion and on other occasions; a shift in emphasis from the major newspapers to news magazines and television as outlets for administration stories; expressed frustration by Kennedy about press coverage; and charges in the press about administration "news management."[13] Perhaps equally telling are the actual practices of reporters covering the major stories of the time, crafting a journalistic language to meet the demands of the facts and the constraints of the genre. At the level of actual practice, we discover considerable variation and an evident frustration with the limits of "objective" reporting.

A reading of the press in the period immediately before, during, and after the Bay of Pigs invasion and the ASNE and ANPA speeches reveals a press experimenting with a variety of methods to frame attributions of motive, structures of appearance versus reality, and states of mind. (For a timeline of the April, 1961, period and later events in U.S.-Cuban relations, see figure 1).

FIGURE 1. TIMELINE: APRIL 1961 AND LATER EVENTS
RELATING TO U.S.-CUBAN RELATIONS

Date	Event
April 15, 1961	Three planes of U.S. manufacture, piloted by Cuban exiles, bomb Cuban air bases.
April 17, 1961	Cuban exile forces invade Cuba, concentrating primarily at the Bay of Pigs. They meet heavy resistance.
April 19, 1961	The last of the more than 1,100 invaders are captured.
April 20, 1961	President Kennedy addresses the American Society of Newspaper Editors
April 21, 1961	President Kennedy holds a televised news conference; he says, "I'm the responsible officer of the Government."
April 25, 1961	President Kennedy and other administration officials hold an off-the-record briefing for the press.
April 27, 1961	President Kennedy addresses the American Newspaper Publishers Association. He urges them, when writing about matters relating to national security, to ask themselves not only "Is it news?" but also "Is it in the interest of national security?"
October 14, 1962	A U.S. spy plane confirms the presence of a ballistic missile on a Cuban launching site.
October 22, 1962	John F. Kennedy addresses a national television audience, announcing a "quarantine" of Cuba to prevent further Soviet supply of Cuban missile systems.
October 28, 1962	Premier Khrushchev agrees to the terms of the quarantine.
December, 1962–July, 1965	The surviving Cuban prisoners from the Bay of Pigs invasion force are ransomed for $53,000,000 in food and medicine.

Newspapers and news magazines in 1961 display a wide variety of means by which to report on other than the official words and deeds of political figures, to interpret those words and deeds by looking behind them, and to use the president as a personification of the United States.

Press coverage of the president and his family makes it clear that there is not a simple, binary division between public and private. Each of these realms partakes of the other. This becomes important for a series of related reasons, showing as it does the centrality of the president to the news process, the seeming accessibility of the president's life to press inspection, and, as we shall see, the depiction of the president's inner life as a frame for understanding his public actions.

John Kennedy was depicted as living part of his personal life in public. For example, on April 16, 1961, the *Boston Globe* printed a photograph of "President and Mrs. Kennedy . . . at Glenwood Park, scene of Middleburg Hunt Race" in a society-page item printed in immediate juxtaposition to the day's political news. Here the "social" links the public with the private; the item gains its importance because it is a photograph of a public figure, and yet the idiom of the photograph might class it as a typical high-society-at-leisure image.[14] In retrospect, at least, the photograph's implications about class and gender seem striking. The Virginia hunt country is clearly the domain of the very rich, and the Hunt Race, as a social occasion, is of importance to the women in the family—Jacqueline Kennedy and the president's sister, Mrs. Jean Smith, also seen in the photograph. Presumably because of his more serious obligations, the "President left before the first race."

Reinforcing the role of the president as the leader of serious public business are further depictions of Mrs. Kennedy as the representative of the feminine, private, social, artistic side of life in the White House. On April 16, Mrs. Kennedy is shown opening a flower show in Washington.[15] On April 12, the *Boston Globe* printed a photograph of Mrs. Kennedy hosting a luncheon for two hundred newspaperwomen. The caption notes that, "In TV news report last night, she expressed hope that daughter, Caroline, 3, would receive less publicity."[16] The television report, broadcast by NBC on April 11, was the second of two documentaries on the Kennedy White House. In one segment of the broadcast,

Sander Vanocur interviews Jacqueline Kennedy, who says that she wants to make the White House a more beautiful museum for people to see, and then, turning to her role as a mother, comments that, "It is rather hard with children. There's so little privacy." When Vanocur asks about life behind the scenes, Mrs. Kennedy accommodates him with a charming story of Ghanaian president Nkrumah, whom she implicitly depicts as crossing the line between public official and family friend by speaking some friendly words to her children.[17]

Jacqueline Kennedy's invitation to share her feelings is enthusiastically taken up by the press. In a report on the White House luncheon, Doris Fleeson writes that, "The fact is that the young chatelaine of the White House is in dead earnest about lightening the mood and temper of living in the formal residence where she is bringing up her two young children."[18] Fleeson's observations underscore the role of the feminine as linked to the family at the same time that they assert the reporter's access to Mrs. Kennedy's inner feelings. We are not told, nor do the journalistic conventions apparently require that we be told, how Fleeson knows for a fact that Mrs. Kennedy is "in dead earnest." In the context of this story, there might seem to be a gendered knowledge at work—one woman knowing what another woman is thinking. Another story on the TV broadcast illustrates how Mrs. Kennedy herself is placed in the self-contradictory position of warning the press away from the president's family at the same time that she shares intimate details of the family and of her own private feelings—making them part of the press agenda. Mrs. Kennedy is quoted as saying that, "I rather hold my breath" about Caroline's going to school, in an article that describes her depicting herself as "anxious."[19]

Press access to Jacqueline Kennedy's feelings sticks to a feminine framework, but access to the inner thoughts of public figures clearly reaches to President Kennedy as well. In an article on Kennedy's costume, Kate Lang ascribes his serious suits to his sense of public obligation: "President Kennedy clearly feels that being well-dressed is part of the simple good manners of public life, and goes at it with a sense of noblesse oblige. Some public figures are personally concerned with clothes almost to the point of fetish. The President leaves it all to [his tailor, Sammie] Harris, who just manages to snatch five minutes for a fitting."[20]

What the president "clearly feels" seems to be on the press agenda throughout the Kennedy years. One generic form that consistently depicts presidential feeling is the news photograph. During the Cuban invasion crisis of April, 1961, for example, the *Boston Globe* printed a close-up of Kennedy with the caption, "A worried President Kennedy will confer with former President Eisenhower today."[21] How the *Globe* knows that the president is "worried," and about what, and how it attaches that worry to the forthcoming meeting with Eisenhower do not need to be stated. On April 29, the *Globe* printed side by side two photographs of Kennedy, one smiling, one more serious. We are invited into his feelings with the caption, "Before and After—President Kennedy, at left, is relaxed and smiling as a candidate. On right, he is shown in a recent photo describing the tenseness of the Laos crisis."[22]

Such interpretive captions were the routine, asserting the power of decontextualized photographs to reveal inner states. In its issue of May 8, 1961, *Newsweek* printed side by side two photographs of congressional leaders Rayburn, Mansfield, McCormack, Albert, and Humphrey, with Vice President Johnson, with the caption, "Guarded grins, unguarded gloom: Congressional leaders posed consciously (left) then were caught unawares (right)." In the "posed" photograph, the men look cheerful; in the "unguarded" photo their faces are serious and Senator Mansfield is shown with his hand across his brow. In the context of a story about the failure of the Cuban invasion, we are invited to regard the photograph of "gloom" as revealing the real feelings of the group.[23] A photograph of Adlai Stevenson describes him as being "thoughtful" as he listens to a U.N. speech by the ambassador from Iraq.[24]

In the NBC White Paper on JFK, the introductory and most significant section of the program was devoted to a behind-the-scenes analysis of how the White House decision-making structures worked, with an emphasis on Kennedy's staff. The very structure of a "behind the scenes" account has significance as a rhetorical move. That a mainstream television network was experimenting with the form helps to underscore how widespread the form was at the time. Seated at the cabinet table,

President Kennedy and his interviewer, Ray Sherer, worked their way through a series of photographs of key White House aides, with Kennedy commenting on the role of each. The most significant moments occur where Scherer expected them to be found when he suggested, "suppose we start with Mr. Sorensen." Kennedy replied that Sorensen was counselor for the White House, with special responsibilities for domestic policies. All attentive observers of the presidency at the time knew of Sorensen's role as Kennedy's speechwriter. Sorensen had been with Kennedy from the start of Kennedy's Senate term in 1953; he was involved in a flurry of public charges—later withdrawn—that he had actually written Kennedy's Pulitzer Prize–winning book *Profiles in Courage;* and he had been Kennedy's primary aide and chief speechwriter in the long campaign for the presidency. The role of speechwriter was known, but it was still—and is today—a somewhat embarrassing aspect of the presidency, since it goes to the center of what we take to be presidential character. Presidential character is displayed to us largely through presidential speeches. At a time when the presidency has become increasingly personalized, it is difficult to find ways to take into account the role of the speechwriter.

In the NBC broadcast, Kennedy appears to have found a euphemistic way to deal with the problem: by telling Scherer that Sorensen's responsibility included the preparation of "messages." "All the messages we send out go through him," says Kennedy. This is literally true, but deflects attention away from the fact that speeches are included among the messages—we don't normally think of speeches as messages that are "sent out." There follows some bantering colloquy between Scherer and Kennedy in which Scherer notes Sorensen's role as alter ego and tells the familiar line that when Kennedy is wounded Sorensen bleeds; Kennedy jokingly replies that Sorensen has even developed a Boston accent, a way of acknowledging their closeness—and the point that Sorensen is clearly subordinate to Kennedy. It is not so much that Kennedy is speaking Sorensen's words as that Sorensen is writing in Kennedy's voice, as an extension and agent of Kennedy.

Kennedy's description of his relationship with Sorensen was consistent with press depictions. In 1961, Alan Otten described Sorensen as close to being an alter ego, as the writer of messages and speeches, but as clearly not a manipulator of Kennedy, whose own strength made him the "senior partner" in the relationship: "In the process of mastering the Kennedy philosophy, Sorensen has also mastered his speaking and writing mannerisms. He can produce on incredibly short notice speeches that express the Kennedy ideas and bear the stamp of Kennedy's style and yet require only minor editing by the President himself before they are delivered."[25]

Otten's description is typical of the way Sorensen was described during the Kennedy administration and in the years since. Kennedy's virtual authorship of his speeches was created not by his briefings of Sorensen, not by his editing of the speeches, but by Sorensen's ability to produce the drafts that Kennedy would have written had he had time to write them. Sorensen's authorship, sometimes obscured, is, even when acknowledged, not regarded as a problem to interpretation since whatever he wrote is what Kennedy would have written. Otten tells a story designed to illustrate Kennedy's entire domination of Sorensen, but it is a story that could be read otherwise: "During the Indiana presidential primary in the spring of 1960 Kennedy's voice gave out and Sorensen was called on to substitute. Reading from papers in his hand, he gave a typical Kennedy campaign speech, including Kennedy-style jokes and some of Kennedy's favorite quotations. Actually, reporters learned later, the papers were blank. The speech came directly from a mind so saturated with Kennedy's thoughts and approach that it could speak perfect Kennedy."[26]

This is an interesting story since it illustrates how Sorensen took the trouble to give the impression that Kennedy had written the words Sorensen was speaking. Even when the trick is revealed, Kennedy remains the controlling rhetorical agent. In this version—one common to our everyday understanding of the rhetorical agency of major political figures—when the president or candidate speaks, he becomes the author. When a spokesman speaks in his place, the president is still the author (though there is a fairly complex grammar of deniability and surrogacy that can be employed in presidential communication). That precisely the reverse could be true in both cases does not enter our minds. This general understanding of the president's agency is an important rhetorical resource. On the other hand, the repetition of such stories may indicate that despite the robustness of the illusion, it requires continuing repair and rebuilding.

As the NBC interview continues, Kennedy explains his preference for a spokes-of-the-wheel staff, reporting to him; he emphasizes his role as a learner and places himself at the center of decision making. "The more people I can see, the wider I can expose to different ideas, the more effective I can be as president." Kennedy's self-depiction as the responsible agent of government is elicited by a question about the role of Richard Neustadt's book *Presidential Power* on the Kennedy White House. Kennedy identifies Neustadt as "an expert on governmental reorganization" and says that the book helps to explain Kennedy's vision of the presidency: "to gather talented people together and constantly stimulate them to action."

Just as Kennedy portrayed himself as the central and controlling agent in the administration, his staff was expected to contribute to that impression, not simply by subordinating themselves to his will but by becoming extensions of that will and agents of his intelligence, adding their own formidable agency to his own. Theodore Sorensen, in his special role as speechwriter, additionally testifies that it was conceived as a primary and routine practice for every presidential speech not merely to advocate policy but also to convey the president's thoughts and intentions clearly and convincingly.[27] And yet, Kennedy was not the sole agent depicted in his speeches; Kennedy also took care to portray his listeners and even absent opponents as autonomous, responsible agents.

President Kennedy spoke to the American Society of Newspaper Editors in the immediate context of the failure of the Bay of Pigs invasion, and in a more general context that made press speculation about presidential thoughts and feelings routine. The press carried into its coverage of the speech and the surrounding political events its assurance that it knew what Kennedy was thinking and feeling.

Theodore Sorensen was charged, as was the usual practice, with planning and preparing the ASNE and ANPA speeches. In an undated memorandum that, again following the usual practice, might have been for Kennedy's decision making, or used as the agenda for a staff meeting, or both, Sorensen suggested possible topics for both speeches. The memo is undated, but the context seems to make it clear that the speeches were planned together as a pair and that the list of topics was prepared before the Bay of Pigs failure made a redrafting of the ASNE speech seem necessary. Although events intruded on the planning, the document does suggest several strategies that were employed in the weeks that followed.

Possible Speech Topics for ASNE—April 20—and Publishers Bureau of Advertising—April 27

1. Relationship between the government and the press— Problems of secrecy and security, orderly and consistent policy, education and public relations, etc.
2. "The education of John Kennedy"—The lessons learned with interest, pain or amusement in the first 100 days.
3. The relationship between our economy and defense—The effect of disarmament on the economy and the budget.
4. The "military-industrial complex"—(Could be included in No. 3 or treated separately).
5. Education—our greatest need—the Administration program.
6. Federal stimulation of research and development for non-defense industries (the Wiesner-Galbraith memo).
7. The world outlook—the challenge we face—etc.[28]

None of these topics appears to anticipate a "crisis speech," which both of the speeches later became. At the same time, several of the themes on the list were used in the ASNE and ANPA speeches and in the background briefings circulated in the following weeks. In the John F. Kennedy Library in Boston there exists an undated document that is apparently Theodore Sorensen's first draft for the ASNE speech. The draft opens with a theme drawn from item number 1 of the planning memo—the relations between government and press, then devotes the remainder of the text to item number 7—the world outlook. The speech draft argues that the American press and government must turn the hopes of the revolution of rising expectations toward the free world by transforming it into a "revolution of increasing satisfactions" through international economic assistance and a domestic agenda that makes America a model for the developing world.

The draft issues a personal challenge to the press and invites them to share responsibility:

> Many of you have written that the American people are apathetic to the dangers which we face—that they are indifferent to the powerful forces which menace the safety of the Great Republic.
>
> I do not believe it. . . .
>
> This then is our responsibility—mine as President, and yours as the interpreters of events to millions of Americans—the responsibility of increasing public awareness of the fact that our civilization is in mortal danger—that our enemies are strong and implacable—that vast and heroic efforts will be required—in short, the responsibility of explaining just what kind of a world we live in.[29]

Sorensen's draft is notable not only for its bold assertion of Kennedy's belief but also for its definition of the world situation as essentially about competing for belief. Although many of the examples in the speech refer to the importance of material development, the essential point of any such development is to secure the allegiance of the world's population to the West. Belief is both the intended action and the manifest subject of the speech.

The failure of the Cuban invasion prompted a redrafting of the ASNE speech. Several versions of Sorensen's new draft of the speech survive in the archives of the John F. Kennedy Library. It is not possible to determine, of course, precisely how much Kennedy himself, or others besides Sorensen, contributed to the shaping of the speech, though it is clear that the redrafting on the eve of the speech would not have been undertaken without Kennedy's direction.

Among the papers on the speech are a handwritten and a typed version of "Introductory Material for ASNE Speech." The separate preparation of a page or two of humorous introductory material was a common practice; such material was usually not included in the advance copy of a speech released to the press, but it typically appeared, if spoken, in the "as actually delivered" press release after the speech, and in the version that appeared in the *Public Papers of the President.* The introductory material refers to Kennedy's appearance at the ASNE convention a year before, when he was considered a long shot for the nomination, behind Adlai Stevenson and Hubert Humphrey. The press's coolness toward him a year before is turned into a self-deprecating joke, in one of Sorensen's trademark balanced constructions: "Also, following my talk here a year ago, I was surprised to find you had no questions—now that I am in office, I am surprised to find how little I have in the way of answers." The text alludes to Kennedy's golf game, turning an Eisenhower-era press complaint about how much time Ike spent on the golf course into a joke on himself: "On the other hand, I realize that your staff and wire service photographers may be complaining that they do not enjoy the same 'green privileges' at the local golf courses, which they once did. It is true that my predecessor did not object, as I do, to pictures of one's golfing skills in action; but neither, on the other hand, did he ever 'bean' a Secret Service man."[30] Given the sobriety of the speech Kennedy gave to ASNE, it seems likely that this material was prepared for the first version of the speech and was discarded as Sorensen undertook a rewrite on the night of April 19. The story then reappears in the April 27 speech to the American Newspaper Publishers Association.

The study of speech preparation in the Kennedy administration is often made more difficult by the very process through which the speeches were composed. Sorensen often composed a first draft of the speech only a few days before delivery—and sometimes in even less time. Although Sorensen occasionally requested suggestions for speech drafts from others within and outside the government, few such suggestions have found their way into the archives. Because Sorensen was so close to Kennedy, because he had access to policy formation, and because he wrote so quickly and so well, there are often few drafts of Kennedy speeches. This creates a difficulty for rhetorical research, since when multiple drafts of a speech are available, it is possible to study the evolution of an intention and, often, the contention among various advisors. In the case of the ASNE speech, though time was very short, we do find several versions of the speech in the archives, and they give some clues to how the final speech was shaped.

Apart from the discarded draft already discussed—which exists in both a handwritten and a typed version—there exist nine further versions of the ASNE speech. These are, in apparent chronological order, based on internal evidence:

1. A handwritten draft, labeled "1st draft." This draft was evidently written on the night of April 19–20, 1961, the night before the speech was to be delivered at 2:00 P.M. on April 20.[31]
2. A typed draft, titled "ASNE SPEECH"; this is a typewritten copy of (1).[32]
3. A copy of (2) with extensive handwritten additions and corrections.[33]
4. A draft titled "2nd draft"; this version is typed, and contains numerous handwritten editorial changes.[34]
5. A cleanly typed version of (4) with two handwritten inserts.
6. A draft titled "3rd draft"; this is a typed version, with further handwritten changes.[35]
7. An advance press-release copy of the speech based on (6).[36]
8. The president's reading copy of the speech, with a few changes in the president's handwriting.[37]
9. "Address before the American Society of Newspaper Editors, April 20, 1961," as printed in the *Public Papers of the President* (1961).

On the evening of April 19, 1961, the night before the ASNE speech, Theodore Sorensen began a completely new version of the speech. President Kennedy, after having met with Sorensen to discuss the matter, attended a reception at the Greek embassy. Sorensen worked through the night on a series of drafts. After midnight, Kennedy met with Lyndon Johnson, secretaries McNamara and Rusk, Admiral Burke, and General Lemnitzer.[38] It is not known whether Sorensen consulted with this group, or with the president alone, during the evolution of the speech that night.

Sorensen's draft makes "identity" a key issue throughout the speech. He begins by identifying the responsibilities of the press with those of the president: "The President of a great democracy such as ours, and the editors of great newspapers such as yours, owe a common obligation to the people: an obligation to present the facts, to present them with candor, and to present them in perspective."

This call on the loyalty of the press is not, on the other hand, met with much candor about the facts of the Cuban invasion, about which the draft says little except to downplay American involvement: "I have emphasized on many occasions that this was a struggle of Cubans against Cubans, of Cuban patriots against a Cuban dictator. While we did not conceal our sympathies, the armed forces of this country have not been involved or committed in any way; nor has anyone who is fully aware of both the diplomatic and military difficulties ever seriously urged a unilateral American intervention to either reinforce or rescue this latest attempt of Cuban refugees and exiles to regain their island's freedom."

The theme of identity and division continues in the next paragraph: "But Cuba is not an island unto itself; and our concern is not ended by mere expressions of non-intervention and regret. This is not the first time in either ancient or recent history that a small band of freedom fighters has been crushed by the armed might of totalitarianism, directed and supplied by an alien power."

American support, which is unspecified, is offered because Cuba is not an isolated entity, and in any case our support is offered on behalf of indigenous (though exiled) forces. The current Cuban regime, on the other hand, is delegitimized since it is "directed and supplied by an alien power."

Could Sorensen and Kennedy reasonably depict the invasion as essentially Cuban? As late as March 15, 1961, McGeorge Bundy advised

Kennedy that the CIA had developed a revised plan for the invasion that was "plausibly Cuban in its essentials."[39]

The difficulties of denying American involvement had been predicted at least as early as February, 1961, in a memo from Arthur M. Schlesinger, Jr., to the president. Schlesinger wrote that in light of just such difficulties, "the arguments *against* this decision begin to gain force. . . . However well disguised any action might be, it will be ascribed to the United States. . . . Worst of all, this would be your first dramatic foreign policy initiative. At one stroke, it would dissipate all the extraordinary good will which has been rising toward the new Administration in the minds of millions."

Schlesinger argued that in the event Kennedy decided to take on the project, he should consider luring Castro into an apparent aggression to which the United States could then respond, or taking on the right-wing dictator Rafael Trujillo "at the same time," thus demonstrating "a principled concern for human freedom." Schlesinger also urged that Kennedy should create a context that would shift the focus:

> Should you not consider at some point addressing a speech to the whole of the hemisphere setting forth in eloquent terms your own conception of inter-American progress toward individual freedom and social justice? Such a speech would identify our Latin American policy with the aspirations of the plain people of the hemisphere. As part of this speech, you could point out the threats raised against the inter-American system by dictatorial states, and especially by dictatorial states under the control of non-hemisphere governments or ideologies. If this were done properly, action against Castro could be seen as in the interests of the hemisphere and not just of American corporations.[40]

In retrospect, it appears that Schlesinger's advice was sound, since the ASNE speech required Kennedy to build a rationale after the fact— a rationale very much along the lines that Schlesinger had suggested in February, emphasizing the illegitimacy of "threats . . . by dictatorial states under the control of non-hemisphere governments."

As events moved toward the invasion, Schlesinger warned again that the United States should prepare its case early—which might have avoided the dramatic, all-night drafting session of April 19–20. In a memo of March 15, Schlesinger advised: "It would seem to me absolutely essential to work out in advance a consistent line which can hold for every conceivable contingency. Otherwise we will find ourselves in a new U-2 imbroglio, with the government either changing its story midstream or else clinging to a position which the rest of the world will regard as a lie."[41]

It is not known whether Sorensen had seen Schlesinger's February memo suggesting the portrayal of the invading forces as loyal Cubans battling a nonhemispheric regime, though the parallels are striking. Sadly, but again perhaps coincidentally, the depictions of the Cuban paramilitary forces for the ASNE speech also echo a more sinister document prepared in the planning phase, a "propaganda action plan" describing possible themes for propaganda leaflets to be dropped over Cuba at the time of the invasion. The "Propaganda Action Plan" suggests:

FIGURE 2. POSSIBLE THEMES FOR D-DAY PERIOD

Cubans reinforcing internal Cuban opposition:	"We" are non-Batista Cubans. We are not foreigners....
Nucleus of original anti-Batista rebels now anti-Castro:	We count among us and among those in hills many who were at Castro's side against Batista's tyranny and who are now fighting Castro's tyranny.
Not an invasion:	This is not an outside, foreign invasion. We are Cubans....

Earlier martyrs paved the way:	We are but the final and crowning Cuban force to crush the Communist dictatorship.
Erase scourge of Communism:	Now that you have felt the heel of a negative Soviet, Asiatic, *foreign,* Communist regime, you know how necessary it is to erase it forever in Cuba.
Respect for Cuban fighters:	Don't let the government call us "imperialists" or "mercenaries." . . .

Source: Annex No. 19, Propaganda Action Plan in Support of Military Forces; Unrestricted; NLK-NSF-CNTRYS-CUBASUBPSRTRANX-4DDDP; Papers of President Kennedy, National Security Files: Countries: Cuba: Subjects, Paramilitary Study Group, Taylor Report, JFKL.

Having established the speech's grammar of identities—the "I," the "we," and the "they"—Sorensen's draft next turns to "lessons for all of us to learn" from "this tragic chain of events." The introduction of the idea of lessons borrows from an idea that had appeared in Sorensen's planning agenda some days before as an idea for the speech to ASNE—but then it was offered, apparently, in more general terms about the education of a president. The notion of lessons in the current draft provides a transition away from an account of what has happened in Cuba in the past days (with the difficulties of assigning responsibility) and invites the audience to consider problems that constrain planning for the future. The shift is from a forensic to a deliberative mode, from self-defense to policy. The three lessons in this first draft are:

1. "that the forces of communism are not to be underestimated";
2. that Cuban communism must be contained and not allowed to spread throughout the hemisphere;

3. "that the communists have made considerable headway . . . in capturing for themselves the 'revolution of rising expectations,' challenging the United States to offer a better route to economic growth and fulfillment."

The third of Sorensen's lessons is drawn from the draft of the now discarded speech. In this new draft, Sorensen tags it with a reflexive gesture to the emergency by noting that "this is the matter on which I had originally planned to talk" (a gesture that is penciled out in the next revision). By the third draft, the third lesson has changed to an entirely different point.

The typed third draft is in nearly final form, though it, too, was further revised with handwritten corrections and additions. In this draft, Kennedy's denial of direct American involvement is overshadowed by his threat to intervene under certain circumstances.

While we could not be expected to hide our sympathies, we made it repeatedly clear that the armed forces of this country would not intervene in any way.

Any unilateral American intervention, in the absence of an external attack upon ourselves or an ally, would have been contrary to our traditions and to our international obligations.[42] But let the record show that our restraint is not inexhaustible. Should it ever appear that the inter-American doctrine of non-interference merely conceals or excuses a policy of non-action—if the nations of this hemisphere should fail to meet their commitments against outside Communist penetration—then I want it clearly understood that this government will not hesitate in meeting its primary obligations which are to the security of our own Nation.

Should that time ever come, we do not intend to be lectured on "intervention" by those whose character was stamped for all time on the bloody streets of Budapest.

The literally accurate but somewhat ambiguous and misleading denial in this passage, claiming in an oddly retrospective hypothetical way that "the armed forces of this country would not intervene in any way" is overshadowed by the strong warning about possible future intervention. The threat of future intervention is used to substantiate the denial of our present involvement, since if the United States did intervene, "we would not expect or accept the same outcome which this small band of gallant Cuban refugees must have known they were chancing." What was originally introduced as a response to an "obligation . . . to discuss briefly at this time the recent events in Cuba" avoids even a general description of American involvement.

To bolster claims of the independence of the Cuban exiles, the speech went through several versions of an account of the leader of the invasion. In his first version Sorensen writes:

> According to press reports, the final message to be relayed from the refugee forces on the island came from the rebel commander when asked if he wished to be evacuated. His answer was: "I will never leave this country." He now joins in the mountains countless other guerrilla fighters, who are equally determined that the dedication of those who gave their lives shall not be forgotten, and that Cuba must not be abandoned to the communists. And we do not intend to abandon it either.

This account disguises American leadership of the invasion by attributing knowledge of the commander's message to "press reports." A passive construction glides past the issue of who would have evacuated the commander had he chosen to withdraw, and of who issued the invitation. The paragraph survives intact into the second draft. The third draft is edited by hand to sharpen the issues of identity with two insertions:

> Mr. Castro has said that these were mercenaries. According to press reports, the final message to be relayed from the refugee forces on the island came from the rebel commander when asked if he wished to be evacuated. His answer was: "I will never leave this country." That is not the reply of a mercenary. He has gone now to join in

the mountains countless other guerrilla fighters, who are equally determined that the dedication of those who gave their lives shall not be forgotten, and that Cuba must not be abandoned to the communists. And we do not intend to abandon it either.

The revised paragraph is characteristic of the speech as a whole in the way it assigns agency to the patriotic rebel leader, at the same time that it disguises U.S. responsibility while staking a claim on the intention of the United States not to "abandon" Cuba.

The draft both implicitly accepts and explicitly rejects responsibility or American involvement, sweeping aside the details with a warning about possible future intervention. Cuba is under the domination of a foreign dictatorship. The rebels are autonomous patriots. The United States, reserving the right to intervene, denies that its armed forces directly intervened in this episode. The account crafted by Sorensen depends for its effect on the rhetorical depiction of human agency, while at the same time sketching the grounds for future American action. Whatever one's views of the invasion, which we now know John F. Kennedy by this time regarded as a dreadful mistake, Sorensen's quickly drafted speech is a subtle work of rhetoric.

Although the denials of American responsibility for the invasion were surely disingenuous, they were, it should be added, used as an implicit explanation for refusing to commit further resources to the battle in such a way as to save face.

The ASNE speech may have redirected press inquiries into Kennedy's and America's involvement in the Bay of Pigs invasion. No causal connection can, of course, be supported, but it does seem that press accounts echo to some degree the themes of identity, responsibility, and lessons that Sorensen crafted in the early hours of April 20, 1961.

Kennedy's ASNE speech was nationally broadcast, widely reprinted, and covered in detail in the press. Coverage quickly coalesced around a series of related themes that placed Kennedy at the center of events.

Time reported on the preparation of the ASNE speech in such a way as to reveal Sorensen's role while emphasizing Kennedy's rhetorical agency. In its April 28 issue, *Time* writers describe how, on the very day that the Cuban invasion failed, Sorensen "worked through the night" at Kennedy's instructions to come up with a "totally different speech" than had earlier been planned. Kennedy is depicted as having decided to make this change, after which he "talked over his ideas with Sorensen until it was time to get ready for the week's second white-tie interruption—a reception at the Greek embassy."[43] Other accounts attributed authorship solely to Kennedy. Don Shannon wrote in the *Los Angeles Times:* "The President, in view of swiftly changing events in Cuba, rewrote his planned speech before the opening luncheon meeting of the ASNE and concentrated on the apparent collapse of the anti-Castro uprising."[44]

Most accounts of the speech implied that the text and its performance provided direct access into Kennedy's state of mind. In a *Los Angeles Times* column objecting to the speech, Holmes Alexander writes that, "President Kennedy, along with his advisors, did not seem to know what kind of policy line the administration was enunciating."[45] Alexander writes that "many of us who listened were disturbed by this 'new' Kennedy—a man visibly feeling the weight and confusion of the office he sought with such vigor and aplomb."[46] Although Alexander reports Kennedy's state of mind, he bases his remarks on direct observation of the president's performance. Some stories reported the president's views without making it clear whether their information came from the speech, background briefings, or other inside knowledge. Robert Healy of the *Boston Globe* writes that "President Kennedy is believed determined to crush the dictatorship of Fidel Castro in Cuba. . . . He has always believed that Castro would have to be dealt with."[47]

Most of the mainstream press appeared to rally to Kennedy's support; those who expressed doubts worried that he might not be tough enough on Cuba. How was a story about a failure by Kennedy and the United States turned into a positive story? Two themes from Kennedy's speech, apparently reinforced by White House background briefings, emerged most clearly—these are the themes of Learning and of Responsibility.

Time interpreted the failed Bay of Pigs invasion as a lesson for President Kennedy, who was "learning . . . the facts of cold war life."[48] The

Boston Globe's report of the ASNE speech describes the president as "grim and determined," and states that, "The President said that we must learn a lesson from Cuba."[49] Taking up the notion that "we" must learn from Cuba, the *Los Angeles Times* accepts the president's speech as an invitation to deliberation. "The President, in his speech to the nation's editors on Thursday, promised that the United States would profit from the lessons of Cuba. What are some of those lessons, and what can be learned from them?"[50] In a more general story on the first 100 days of the administration, John Hightower, though critical of Kennedy, depicts him as a learner. "At the heart of all of Kennedy's major problems, of course, was the nature of his relations with [Nikita] Khrushchev. On this point, some of his aides and advisors, if not Kennedy himself, seem to have been surprised, even shocked, at the violent, uncompromising nature of the cold war seen from inside the government."[51]

The theme of Kennedy as a learner is part of a thread that runs through press coverage not only of the Cuban story but also of the administration as a whole, and that depends for its effect on getting inside the president's head. Kennedy is depicted both as a learner and as a uniquely situated observer of events. Inside information about the rising or falling stock of Kennedy's colleagues is fertile ground for confidently retailed gossip about the president's views. *Newsweek* mentioned, for example, that "President Kennedy is immensely pleased with Vice President Johnson's record as good-will ambassador and plans to expand these duties."[52] In the wake of the Cuban failure, as blame became attached to Allen Dulles, director of the CIA, *Newsweek* revealed that "JFK has no idea yet, but wistfully wishes he had another trusted brother like Attorney General Bobby to fill the vital post [of Director of CIA]."[53]

In the days after the Cuban invasion, the issue of who was responsible flashed through the press. Kennedy assumed responsibility from the outset. At his press conference on April 21, Kennedy was asked by Sander Vanocur, "In view of the fact we are taking a propaganda lambasting around the world, why is it not useful, sir, for us to explore with you the real facts behind this, or our motivations?" Curiously, Kennedy turned a question that seemed directed at national purposes into a question about his personal role. Kennedy replied, in part, that "we have to make a judgment as to how much we can usefully say that would aid the interest of the United States. One of the problems of a free society, a problem not met by a dictatorship, is this problem of information. . . . There's an old saying that victory has 100 fathers and defeat is an orphan. . . . I have said as much as I feel can usefully be said by me in regard to the events of the past few days. Further statements, detailed discussions, are not to conceal responsibility because I'm the responsible officer of the Government—that is quite obvious—but merely because I do not believe that such a discussion would benefit us during the present difficult situation."[54]

Kennedy's direct assumption of responsibility in his reply to Sander Vanocur's question could be construed, in hindsight, as less than entirely satisfactory, since after the ambiguous denials of the ASNE speech it is not entirely clear for what it is that President Kennedy is claiming to be responsible. Kennedy meets this problem, in part, by his observation that further elaboration would not "benefit us during the present difficult situation," and by his reminder that a democracy faces special difficulties when confronted by an adversary that does not have a free press. From a rhetorical point of view, Kennedy's assumption of responsibility seems to have been a success.

Nevertheless, rumors circulated that Allen Dulles had given bad advice. Interior Secretary Stewart Udall was quoted as saying that the invasion plan was originally Richard Nixon's, agreed to by Eisenhower, and inherited by Kennedy. In the face of an immediate outcry from Republicans, President Kennedy issued a statement personally assuming full responsibility for the failure. Although this story was told by the press, Kennedy was generally given credit for taking the responsibility, even by the opposition. In a story soon after the invasion, the *Boston Globe* editorialized that, "President Kennedy, who has refused to shun the onus, is burdened with an outcome whose chief cause roots in an old source," which it finds in the CIA.[55]

Some of the reports of Kennedy's assumption of responsibility frame it as a story of "ulterior motives." On April 25, Don Shannon, in the *Los*

Angeles Times, writes that "President Kennedy, moving to halt a bipartisan battle over blame for the Cuban disaster, Monday night issued 'sole responsibility for the events of the past days' and ordered officials not to attempt to implicate the Eisenhower administration."[56] Shannon's story is a switch from his earlier frame for the event; on April 22, he had written that, "Looking worn by the continuous round of high level conferences which followed the rebel defeat, he wryly observed: 'There is an old saying that victory has 100 fathers and defeat is an orphan.'"[57] The *Boston Globe,* generally a strong Kennedy paper, interpreted the taking of responsibility as sincere on its face. On the front page, the administration press release is interpreted as merely repeating what Kennedy had said from the outset: "President Kennedy, reaffirming his full responsibility for the United States setback on Cuba, tonight ordered members of his official family not to try to shift the blame to anyone else."[58] An unsigned story on the inside pages of the *Globe* casts the story in the same way: "President Kennedy has again made it clear that he takes full responsibility for whatever part the United States played in the Cuban invasion." The *Globe* story then quotes the press release: "President Kennedy has stated from the beginning that as President he bears sole responsibility for the events of the past few days. He has stated it on all occasions and he restates it now so that it will be understood by all. . . . The President is strongly opposed to anyone within or without the administration attempting to shift the responsibility."[59]

As if to reinforce the sincerity of Kennedy's assumption of responsibility, some reporters emphasized how deeply he was shocked and shaken. James Reston wrote that, "For the first time in his life, John F. Kennedy has taken a public licking. He has faced illness and even death in his 43 years, but defeat is something new to him, and Cuba was a clumsy and humiliating defeat, which makes it worse. . . . How he reacts to it may very well be more important than how he got into it."[60]

Edwin Lahey and David Kraslow pursued Reston's theme in the *Boston Globe,* identifying the nation strongly with Kennedy and seeing in his reaction to events a test of character. "We made our purpose known publicly, in an agonizing burst of honesty, after John F. Kennedy for the first time in his 43 years felt the acrid taste of complete and humiliating defeat.... The taste of defeat was bitter to the President. All the Kennedys play to win, whether the game is parchesi or the balance of terror in a world armed for destruction.... Mr. Kennedy picked himself up off the mat, figuratively speaking, even while he was going through the motions of ceremonial graciousness with members of Congress and their wives."[61]

Writing in the *Los Angeles Times,* its Washington bureau chief Robert T. Hartmann links the president's responsibility to his special knowledge. Although he was a Nixon supporter, Hartmann extends to Kennedy the unique perspective and responsibility of the office. He writes that "the man who lives in the White House is not governed by what he would like to do or by the words that are necessary to win debates or elections. Whoever he is, he is governed by the inexorable facts of the world as it is and by the over-riding national interest, which becomes apparent only to those who sit at the pivot point of America's destiny."[62]

In a later story, Hartmann claims knowledge of what is on Kennedy's mind and avoids choosing between personal and shared responsibility for the Cuban invasion. "The Kennedy administration appears to be taking the position that the Cuban fiasco was a bipartisan blunder initiated under President Eisenhower and endorsed by his top advisers, including intelligence and military chiefs who have continued in their posts. . . . At the same time President Kennedy is personally accepting full responsibility for the decision to go ahead with the ill-fated rebel reinforcement operation. He is both aware and angry that some subordinate U.S. officials are claiming that they knew nothing of it or counseled against it."[63]

It is difficult to know exactly how to read Hartmann's story. The most plausible interpretation of what Hartmann is leading us to appears to be that Kennedy is sincerely determined to spread bipartisan blame while gaining credit for appearing to accept responsibility. This strategic reading is certainly within the powers of Hartmann, who was later a special counsel to President Gerald Ford, and whose brief included political strategy and final editorial responsibility for speeches.

Hartmann had a sharply developed sense of the conspiratorial ener-
gies swirling through the White House. In his later book on the Ford
presidency, *Palace Politics* (1980), Hartmann blamed the troubles of the
Ford administration on Nixon holdovers, whom he characterized as a
"palace guard."[64]

The problem with the responsibility theme, of course, is that those
papers most willing to accept Kennedy's claims of responsibility at face
value are his supporters who are most willing also to accept the idea
that part of the blame is bipartisan; those opposed to Kennedy are most
likely to read his claim of responsibility as true but insincere.

The themes of learning, responsibility, personnel, and surveillance
are neatly tied together in a *Washington Post* column by Carroll
Kilpatrick, who writes that Robert Kennedy and Theodore Sorensen
have been asked, in the aftermath of the Cuban invasion, to advise
President Kennedy on foreign policy, not because they are foreign policy
experts but because "they must help him consider every foreign policy
problem in terms of its effect on the President's own authority and
prestige—as well as the Nation's." Kilpatrick traces this decision to the
doctrines in Richard Neustadt's book *Presidential Power*. Neustadt, who
was then a special assistant to Kennedy, argued that every decision by
a president must be considered with an eye on "the importance of success, and the necessity always to think in terms of the effect of actions
on the high office he holds."[65]

Kilpatrick takes us behind the scenes of the presidency, but in a way
that instead of inducing suspicion at the politics of illusion links the
president's success with that of the nation. While there is surely room
in the Kilpatrick-Neustadt version of the presidency for suspicion of
the president's motives, this is clearly not the interpretation to which
Kilpatrick invites his readers. This, it seems to me from reading doz-
ens of press accounts of the failed Cuban invasion and Kennedy's reaction to it, is the burden of depictions both pro and con—that the
presidency is a unique resource for the nation, that the character and
routines of the president are crucial to his success and to ours, and that
all assistance to the president, including ghostwriting, is transformed
into the president's personal action when it flows through him.

In its coverage of the Bay of Pigs invasion, the press accepted President Kennedy's assumption of responsibility as a sign of character, and it accepted the idea that the invasion had lessons to teach as an indication that, even if Kennedy had made a mistake, he was capable of learning from it. Although the theme of ulterior motives was clearly available to the press in April, 1961, it was largely avoided. But the rhetorical foundation of the ulterior motive theme was being laid. The press had a well-developed vocabulary of appearance vs. reality, actions vs. motives, words as the sign of inner states, and the personalization of the presidency. In the case of the Bay of Pigs invasion, this vocabulary was employed largely to support the president as the personification of the interests of the United States. All of these themes, which were employed to convey positive news about President Kennedy, were readily available to have their valence changed from positive to negative when Vietnam and Watergate undermined trust in presidential leadership.

CHAPTER 3

In the National Interest

The Speech to the American Newspaper Publishers Association

In the week following John F. Kennedy's speech to the American Society of Newspaper Editors (ASNE), the press followed Kennedy's framing of the story as one of responsibility assumed and lessons learned. Even in the midst of the Cuban story, other events crowded the front pages: French president Charles de Gaulle defeated a revolt of French colonial generals in Algeria who had planned to invade France itself; and battles in Laos threatened to intensify the cold war and draw the United States into a Southeast Asian war. Kennedy retained and extended the themes of the ASNE speech a week later, on April 27, 1961, in his speech to the American Newspaper Publishers Association (ANPA). The ANPA speech returned to the theme of the president and the press, which had been touched on in the ASNE speech. But in the ANPA speech Kennedy set off a largely negative response by urging editors and publishers to ask of any potential story touching on national security not only "Is it news?" but also "Is it in the national interest?"

The Kennedy administration was closely involved with the press in the aftermath of the Cuban invasion, with the speech to ASNE, a Kennedy press conference the next day, and an off-the-record briefing on April 25. In addition, there appears to have been a fairly heavy schedule of background briefings for individual reporters. Kennedy meetings with Eisenhower, Nixon, Rockefeller, and other Republican leaders produced pictures and stories on the front pages.

The only references to the April 25 briefing are in indirectly attributed press reports; for many years, it appeared that the White House kept no official transcript. The way the White House handled that briefing shows something about how the administration managed its relations with the press. A memorandum in the John F. Kennedy Library lists a series of speeches by Kennedy that were not published in *The Public Papers of the President*. Among those not published is "Off-the-Record Remarks—Editors and Columnists State Department Briefing, New State Department Auditorium," April 25, 1961.[1] John Romagna, whose job it was to transcribe Kennedy's speeches, had apparently made no copy of this briefing. Kennedy's speeches were either recorded on audio tape and made available to the news media, usually in an advance press release of the speech as prepared and a followup, corrected press release transcribing the speech "as actually delivered," or fell into one of five other categories:

(A) Not recorded by anyone.
(B) No tape.
(C) No transcript made, or rough draft is in Romagna's file.
(D) Transcribed for White House historical record only; not given to Press, except as they covered it on the spot.
(E) Transcribed for White House historical record only. Not given to Press, who did NOT cover the event.[2]

The April 25 briefing is listed in the Romagna index as belonging to category C, for which "no transcript [was] made or [for which the] rough draft is in Romagna's file." There is no rough draft of the remarks in Romagna's file, so from the perspective of this authoritative list, it appears that no transcript was made, evidently because the administration was concerned about security, but also to manage the transmission of John Kennedy's utterances. For example, Kennedy did speak about Cuba at his April 21 news conference, but primarily to say that he did not think it wise to comment in detail. Kennedy's most forceful statement assuming responsibility for the government's involvement was issued in a press release rather than in an oral statement to the press or public.

Other considerations seem to have governed the nonpublication of the other items from the Romagna index, most of which do not appear to present any particular security issues. It is perhaps worth observing for students of rhetoric that among the Kennedy utterances that rose to the level of "speeches" but that were not included in the public papers, the record lists forty-eight items for 1961. The exclusion of these fairly trivial items, at the rate of about one a week, illustrates how the depiction of Kennedy's views and his level of eloquence was managed for the press at the time and for the historical record as it appears in *The Public Papers of the President.*

But in fact John Romagna did make a transcript of the off-the-record press briefing of April 25. This transcript was among a large number of boxes of Pierre Salinger's records kept sealed to public access for security reasons until July 8, 1997. The discovery of the transcript of the April 25 press briefing makes it possible to see how much Sorensen was drawing on a series of statements by Kennedy himself when he composed the ANPA speech.

Kennedy had spoken about the press and national security at his very first presidential press conference, long before the Cuban invasion became a salient part of the issue—though accounts of the training camps had appeared, and worried the administration. In his first press conference, on January 25, 1961, Kennedy was asked several questions about his relations with the press and about freedom of information. One reporter questioned the live TV broadcasting of the press conference:

Q. Mr. President, there has been some apprehension about the instantaneous broadcast of Presidential press conferences such as this one, the contention being that an inadvertent statement no longer correctible, as in the old days, could possibly cause some grave consequences. Do you feel that there is any risk or could you give us some thought on that subject?

THE PRESIDENT. Well, it was my understanding that the statements made by the, by President Eisenhower, were on the record. There may have been a clarification that could have been issued afterwards but it still would have demonstrated, it still would have been on the record as a clarification, so that I don't think that the interests of our country are—it seems to me that they're as well protected under this system as they were under the system followed by President Eisenhower. And this system has the advantage of providing more direct communication.[3]

A few moments later, a reporter asked about information and national security.

Q. Mr. President, Press Secretary Salinger said today, indicated today, there might be a need for a tightening of information on national security. Doesn't the policy of deterrence require that the enemy have knowledge of our strength and the ability to carry them out and wouldn't there be a risk of possible miscalculation by tightening up information?

THE PRESIDENT. Well, I think that the enemy is informed of our strength. I think Mr. Salinger in his statement today at lunch indicated his judgment based on his experience so far, that there had been very ample information given so that the enemy can make a determination as to our strength. I am anxious that we have a maximum flow of information but there quite obviously are some matters which involve the security of the United States, and it's a matter on which the press and the Executive should attempt to reach a responsible decision.

I could not make a prediction about what those matters will be, but I think that all of us here are aware that there are some matters which it would not be well to discuss at particular times so that we just have to wait and try to work together and see if we can provide as much information as we can within the limits of national security. I do not believe that the stamp "National Security" should be put on mistakes of the administration which do not involve the national security, and this administration would welcome any time that any member of the press feels that we are artificially invoking that cover. But I must say that I do not hold the view that all matters and all information which is available to the Executive should be made available at all times, and I don't think any member of the press does. So it's a question of trying to work out a solution to a sensitive matter.[4]

These remarks at the January press conference make it clear, and would have made it clear to the Washington press corps, that the issue of press restraint had been on Kennedy's mind from the very beginning of his administration, and that he did not raise the matter in the ANPA speech simply as a way of deflecting attention from the failure of the Bay of Pigs invasion.

On April 25, just two days before the ANPA speech, Kennedy appeared at the background briefing for which the transcript is now available. In thirty-one minutes, Kennedy laid out a remarkably lucid, confident, and thoughtful appraisal of the aftermath of the Cuban invasion and its place in U.S. policy. He touched on issues of the press at several points, remarking in his opening comments that in various guerrilla wars around the world the communist forces "are able to operate anonymously. Everything we do is printed in the paper; and they are carrying on their struggles with all of the advantages of secrecy."[5]

At one point, in response to a question about press coverage of the Cuban invasion, Kennedy made an answer that appears to be both an important source for Sorensen's text of his speech to ANPA two days later and a rationale for not making the speech. A reporter asked:

Q. Mr. President, the argument has been made that the very strength of the reporting on the preparations for the Cuban invasion indicated how much leakage and how much faction-ridden this operation was, and it should have been a warning that it was an ill-founded one.

On the other hand, the argument was made that the press did a disservice by the extent of its reporting. Have you given any thought to what is the role of the press in covering para-military warfare?

THE PRESIDENT: Well, I hope the press will consider it. It's very difficult for a public official to discuss this matter, because it is a sensitive matter.

The press is rightfully concerned with any efforts to limit its reporting of events. The press, however, is a Fourth Estate, and therefore in a sense has important public responsibilities. It seems to me that it's a matter which the press should consider.

I think, if you go over the reports which have been made in recent weeks—many of them inaccurate—many of the reports coming out of Miami were inaccurate. Others were accurate, coming out of different areas, and which were extremely damaging to us.

If we were attempting to carry on any other operations in this or other areas, the next day, or even once we made a decision, undoubtedly it would be printed in the paper. And any preparations which were made would be printed in the paper.

One paper did carry a very carefully detailed analysis of the business about the defecting pilots, as to how the story couldn't possibly be true, one, two, three, four, at a time when we were under attack at the United Nations.

Now, this is a matter that you gentlemen have to decide in this kind of a cold war, what you should print and what you should not print.

I, of course, have thoughts about it. But I must say it seems to me that this is an area where you ought to make your judgments, and perhaps consider it almost as a profession, not merely individually. Because we are going to have, I hope, not a similar situation, but other situations which will require us to complete any preparations we make, and before we carry them on, and you reporters can always determine what is going on here.[6]

The discovery of the off-the-record Kennedy background conference is a significant addition to the historical record, and it offers a useful tool when considering the rhetoric of presidential speechmaking. A comparison of the status of the off-the-record conference with the ANPA speech demonstrates something of the complexity of both as speech acts. Clearly the news conference is partly the basis for the ANPA speech two days later. But why was the speech necessary? Not simply to set an agenda and not even to reveal the president's thoughts. The press had already begun to reflect on its own role in the Bay of Pigs. Kennedy's discussion of the issue at his backgrounder could not be directly attributed to him, but the press now had the matter on its own agenda. Further, the press conference not only communicated the idea of press self-censorship as an idea, but also convincingly revealed that Kennedy wanted them to consider the idea. Indeed, for Kennedy to urge restraint when he was off the record might mark his utterance as particularly his own, as not having been through the hands of a speechwriter, a particularly important consideration when the rhetoric of attribution was so important a part of press coverage of the presidency. But Kennedy answered only the second half of the reporter's question, relating to press responsibility, not the first half, as to whether the press revealed weaknesses in the operation that should have led the administration to call it off. A reporter could not know whether Kennedy's emphasis on the half of the question relating to the press was spontaneous, or, on the contrary, an opportunistic move to a theme he had already planned to talk about. It would be a false dichotomy to assume that speeches were mostly ghostwritten and press conferences mostly spontaneous. Both forms involved mixed modes of authorship and agency. Before important press conferences, President Kennedy typically read briefing books, which posed possible questions and suggested answers—and the press certainly knew that.

When the president urged press restraint in public and on the record, as he did in the ANPA speech on April 27, he was therefore not doing so merely to put the matter on the agenda, and not merely to inform the press that he thought they ought to consider it. They already knew that. Nor was Kennedy merely repeating himself. Most obviously, in the ANPA speech Kennedy develops the idea of press restraint more fully and more eloquently, giving it a context and an argumentative structure. In addition, in speaking in public and on the record, the president stages a drama for a larger audience. At the background conference, Kennedy was, in terms of the drama of the event, engaged in a dialogue with the press. In a sense, the ANPA speech was also a dialogue with the press, but in this case the dialogue was taking place on a public stage, casting the press as public actors and speaking over their heads to the nation. In speaking in public, Kennedy was speaking on the record, meaning that he was not merely *communicating* ideas to the press for their consideration but also *committing* himself to having uttered those ideas and in effect requiring them, as the background conference did not do, to make some sort of response or to be seen, themselves, as avoiding the issue. A presidential speech, for better or worse, can thus be seen as a peculiar sort of speech act, not merely an argument but a drama of commitment, leveraging power through the act of committing a president to the record. To be sure, the differences in rhetorical status of a background news conference and a presidential speech are implicit, but that they are implicit does not diminish their ability to inflect the narrative of what the president's talk represents and what it is doing.

The speech to the American Newspaper Publishers Association had been scheduled since before the Cuban invasion, but appears to have been addressed to the perceived exigencies of the crisis. Almost three weeks before the ANPA speech, Arthur Schlesinger forwarded to Sorensen a memorandum describing a message from Dorothy Schiff of the *New York Post,* reminding Schlesinger that Kennedy was scheduled to speak to the Bureau of Advertising of the ANPA, and that it was "essentially a dinner of advertising people." He quotes Schiff: "I have noted in other years that the speaker always seems to be under the impression that he is addressing the editorial-side people—influential writers and molders of public opinion—rather than advertising people. Of course, when the speaker is as important as a President of the U.S., many more publishers will attend than normally, but on the whole the dinner is chiefly attended by business office people. Very few, if any, editors, for instance, ever are there."[7]

This memorandum is significant because it makes clear that if Kennedy wished to avoid the tangle of issues presented by the Cuban crisis, he could do so on the implicit grounds that the ANPA audience was composed of "business office people," for whom a speech on business issues or even an after dinner or ceremonial address could be made to seem entirely appropriate. Kennedy's decision to raise a substantive and controversial issue, as if he were addressing editors and publishers, is therefore revealed as a deliberate tactic. Even so, the tactic may have been intended as either or both of two distinct modes of address, that is, either an appeal over the heads of the press to the listening public, or an appeal to the audience of editors and publishers implied by the text. But the question of voice and audience was to become still more complex as the press became in tangled ways the source, the subject, and the audience for the speech.

The recollections of Pierre Salinger, Kennedy's press secretary, help us to understand the development of the ANPA speech. Press reactions to Kennedy's ASNE speech on April 20 indicate a press that, though critical, is willing to give Kennedy the benefit of the doubt on a foreign policy failure. Salinger, however, recalls that at the time he and Kennedy regarded press response to the Cuban invasion as strongly negative and a cause for concern.

Salinger recalls that immediately after the April 21 press conference, Kennedy was angry at Sander Vanocur's question about Cuba, and that he was even more angry the next morning when the press criticized him for not saying more in his response. When Kennedy said that the press needed to understand the importance of secrecy in some areas of foreign policy, Salinger recalls suggesting that the upcoming speech to ANPA would be a good occasion to address the issues involved. Kennedy agreed and instructed Salinger to send his ideas on the matter to Sorensen.[8]

Salinger recalls that his advice to Kennedy to speak on press restraint was a suggestion that he "would later regret. . . . I had," writes Salinger, "given JFK bad advice."[9] Salinger in retrospect argues that the speech was faulty not so much in its substance as in its timing, which made it appear that Kennedy was seeking to silence the press just when the failure of the Cuban adventure made public scrutiny seem especially important.

Research in the JFK Library has not yet turned up a copy of a Salinger memo of April 22, to Sorensen. It may be that the memo has been lost, or it may be that Salinger has the chronology slightly askew, since there is a memo from Salinger to Sorensen dated April 17, 1961. The April 17 memo, on "The relations of the President with the press" seems to be background material for a possible speech, and we do know that Sorensen had been considering such a topic for either the ASNE or the ANPA speeches.

Salinger's April 17 memo is a peculiar document, part a backgrounder for Sorensen on the White House press corps; part a list of grievances about the press corps; and part a thematic list of what appear to be possible points to raise in a presidential speech on press-presidency issues. Salinger describes the growth of the press corps from two hundred accredited reporters in Franklin Roosevelt's White House to one thousand in the Kennedy White House. Roosevelt's intimate, off-the-record meetings with the press were attended by fifty reporters; in the Kennedy administration, more than four hundred attended.

Kennedy had introduced live television to his press conferences, causing some complaints among the print reporters, but Salinger asserts that "the present format is here to stay. . . . Television has not basically altered the character of the Press Conference. And the admittance of television to the press is only simple justice. To allow other media to use their tools to the fullest extent and to deny this same right to the radio and television industry is in my opinion the grossest of injustice."[10] Salinger may be right about the justice of allowing the television media access to the press conferences, but his analysis of the communicative implications of the change seems one-sided. We have learned in the years since the Kennedy administration that a long press conference, televised live, can combine two incompatible forms. On the one hand, the press is attempting to elicit answers that can, individually, be used as quotations in a story. On the other hand, once it is accessible to live television, a press conference becomes a drama in which we can see press and president (or press secretary) enacting the adversarial theater of Washington journalism. The press in the Kennedy period sometimes complained that the president used the press conference to speak over their heads. Salinger acknowledges a different line of complaint from the press—that their normal practices, suited to newsgathering, look improper in the context of a live press conference, thus diminishing their credibility and pressuring them to alter their proven methods. Salinger tells Sorensen:

> But the admission of television to the press conference has done something else—and here we may find the explanation for the current press preoccupation with the character of the conference. It has opened up to full view of 60,000,000 people the workings of the American reporter. And the fact is that the people are not particularly enchanted with what they see. They consider the reporters rude, their questions inept. In fairness to the reporters, it should be noted that their questions are no better or worse than they have been in the past. For the first time, however, they are subjected to a critical eye. Reporters are not rude. Their method of attempting to gain recognition is time honored and nobody in Washington (including the President) gives this a second thought. It is true that to the untrained eye they may appear rude, but the public cannot be considered experts on the behavior of reporters.[11]

Salinger concluded his memo with a series of observations that he apparently offered as themes for a Sorensen speech draft. Virtually all of them were posed as defenses of the administration's record in press relations.

1. We believe in the complete right of the press to know what is going on in government within the confines of national security. To this end we have instituted a program which I think has made commendable steps in this direction. Congressman John Moss, Chairman of the House Subcommittee on Freedom of Information, declared in Seattle Friday night that this Administration has brought about the "most significant developments we have seen in the long fight for freedom of information."

2. We have made major strides in our relationships with foreign correspondents. This is vital not only to this Administration but to the nation since people in foreign countries get their impression of America from foreign correspondents of newspapers, radio and TV stationed in this country.

3. We have made major steps in the area of coordination of government policy. This is not to say we are attempting to dry up sources of information but rather to present a broader picture of what the government is doing. Coordination among Departments is responsible, in my opinion, for the successful handling of the RB-47 incident and other less important matters.

4. We have instituted the most extensive background briefing sessions for Presidential messages ever developed in Washington. Previous Administrations convened White House background sessions for only the budget and economic messages. Cabinet officials and other top government personnel have participated in some 15 briefing sessions held at the White House.

5. The Presidential press conference has been opened up for the people to see and hear through television and radio. We have received literally thousands of letters in support of this move from people around the country who want to see the President in action.

6. People have been given a new dimension of the Presidency and the President. The President is no longer a mysterious figure operating behind closed doors.

7. The President has been greatly accessible to the press and while this has been on a selected basis it is still extremely effective in communicating his views to the people of influence in the newspaper profession.[12]

Even if all of these points were true—and several were considered debatable at the time—they are not especially useful for the composition of a presidential speech addressed to the press and overheard by the public. These are virtually all boasts about presidential accomplishments, and most of them are implicitly posed as refutations to allegations made by someone in the press. To build a speech around them would certainly have seemed to diminish the president, casting him as a boastful and antagonistic figure at the level of a press corps that was implicitly cast as griping and unreasonable. As a report from Salinger to Sorensen on how well he had been doing his job, the report was credible, but as a draft for a presidential speech, the Salinger memorandum was transparently a piece of press-agentry. Sorensen could perhaps use the material as background on the mood and the concerns of the press and the press secretary, but it would be unwise to draw the president into a full-scale debate with the press, especially in the midst of the Cuba story.

Salinger had been working on the question of freedom of information since the earliest days of the administration; his public activities in responding to issues of freedom of information and charges of news management had put these matters on the agenda long before the Cuban invasion and the ANPA speech.

On March 8, 1961, Salinger spoke to the Publicity Club of Chicago, where he bluntly claimed that, "Access to information at the White House today is freer than it has ever been before. The people of this country are getting a dimension of the Presidency they have never received before." Salinger's defensiveness is palpable, and is directed as much at leakers within the government as at journalists who were taking advantage of such leaks. Salinger said that,

Information is the life blood of our society—and without it we will not survive. It has been said—and rightly so—that secrecy is the first refuge of incompetents. But today the issues are much more complicated than just secrecy—it involves in some cases the management of news, in others the timing of news to fit particular political necessities.

Let me say this bluntly—America would not have the serious problems it has today were it not for the fact that in the past years the people have not been given the facts.

Any Administration which allows free access to information is also going to reveal to the public internal debates on policy. This is inevitable. . . . I think we want our government to be a seat of ideas, a place for healthy debate. Once the policy is arrived at, however, with everyone having their say, then in my opinion the necessity is there for complete support of this policy by all spokesmen for the Administration. . . .

. . . I am a strong advocate of freedom of information—within the confines of national security. . . .

So freedom and responsibility must stand side by side. Freedom without responsibility is anarchy.[13]

On April 19, 1961, Salinger's office released an exchange of letters between Salinger and E. S. Pulliam, Jr., managing editor of the *Indianapolis News*. Pulliam, writing as chair of an ASNE committee on freedom of information, had addressed a detailed letter to Salinger on February 15, claiming that, "As I am sure you are aware, there has been considerable publicity, speculation, and criticism of various aspects of public information during the early days of the Kennedy administration." Pulliam listed nine "events [that] have caused concern" and asked Salinger to respond in writing.[14] Salinger responded on April 18; his office released both his and Pulliam's letters on April 19, the day before the ASNE speech and just a week before the ANPA speech. The timing of these events would surely have made the press highly attentive to anything the administration might have to say about freedom of information.

Sorensen was committed to developing a speech on the presidency and the press and in the middle of a busy week had only a few days to come up with something. He had some material that he had discarded in the rewrite of the ASNE speech. He had some additional material that had accumulated in the first months of the administration with a developing debate about news management, freedom of information, and national security.

Salinger's was not the only advice Kennedy received on the ANPA speech. Sorensen and Kennedy, though the time was short, had other alternatives. On April 22, the same day that Salinger recalls talking with

Kennedy on the morning after the press conference, McGeorge Bundy sent Sorensen a memo suggesting "a major NATO speech," and including a "draft of elements" for such a speech. April is the anniversary month for NATO, making such a speech ritually timely. Furthermore, Bundy argued that the timing was right because of the damage to the alliance caused by the Cuban failure. "The more I think about it, the more I believe that the general theme of this speech is just right for Thursday. I saw Harold Caccia last night, and he believes that nothing would do more at this stage to relight our candle with our allies, after Cuba."[15]

But Sorensen and Kennedy proceeded with plans to make a speech about the press. On Monday, April 24, Sorensen received a note from Lester Markel, the Sunday editor of the *New York Times*. Markel writes, "Here are some additional notes the President suggested. I trust you will find them useful."[16] Stapled to this note, and a note of thanks from Sorensen to Markel dated May 2, are two pages of text for the ANPA speech. It appears that the two pages were written by Markel, though it is not impossible that these were Sorensen draft materials that had been sent to Markel for comment, or that they are simply Sorensen pages that found their way into the bundle, or even that they were all or part of the undiscovered memo Salinger recalls writing on April 22. But if the pages were written by Markel, as seems likely, then it is clear now that the most offensive passages of the ANPA speech had their origin in Markel's draft. It may seem peculiar, to say the least, that any presidential speech, much less a speech on press restraint, should be based in part on a draft written by a newspaper editor. But the practice, though not routine, was by no means unprecedented. On at least several occasions, the Kennedy administration seems to have asked writers such as Arthur Krock, Walter Lippmann, and Norman Cousins for speech materials.

The *Times* itself was in the midst of sorting out a debate among its own editors and reporters about its coverage of the Cuban invasion. The *Times* had been reporting since January on the training camps for Cuban exiles in the jungles of Guatemala, though the story had apparently been broken by *The Nation* in November, 1960, in the waning days of the Eisenhower administration. James Reston recalls that on April 6, *Times* reporter Tad Szulc sent a story from Miami in which he said that a Cuban invasion was "imminent." *Times* editors Ted Bernstein and Lew Jordan made the story the next day's lead, under a four-column headline, but in an unusual move managing editor Turner Catledge overruled them. "Catledge eliminated the *imminent* and the references to the CIA, and cut the headline down to one column, and Bernstein and Jordan were furious."[17] Reston reports that the incident was controversial among journalists, especially at the *Times,* for years, with sharply opposed camps arguing on the one hand that it was the responsibility of the paper to report the news, which might have headed off the invasion, and on the other hand that it was not the business of the paper to publish speculative material in order to influence national policy. Although Lester Markel does not appear to have been directly involved in the editing of the Szulc story, he would surely have known about the controversy, and because of his special role as editor of the Sunday paper might have been expected to favor the introduction of interpretation into the news pages. But his draft for the ANPA speech argues forcefully for patriotic restraint. Perhaps this is explained by Reston's memory of Markel as a "talented, grumpy martinet," and of the editors as devoting "most of their time to their separate responsibilities and the rest of their time to criticizing one another."[18] Markel is recalled by various *Times* writers as grumpy, demanding, irascible, and as an excellent editor. He was Sunday editor of the *Times* from 1923 to 1964; after World War II, Markel founded the International Press Institute as an advocate of worldwide press freedom. And so, given the turmoil at the *Times,* if Kennedy and Sorensen thought that they were avoiding trouble by clearing an appeal for press responsibility with a representative of the press, they miscalculated, walking instead into the midst of a controversy they could easily have avoided, and in which they were predictably met with indignation by a significant segment of the press.

Lester Markel sent two notes to the White House on April 24. The first, addressed to the president directly, indicates that Markel and Kennedy had talked the previous Friday about the ANPA speech:

Dear Mr. President:

Here, as requested, are those notes I promised for the talk to the publishers. They present only the argument and they are rough, but I hope they will be of some use. Ted Sorensen, I am sure, can add meat, logic and eloquence to them.

I was heartened when I saw you Friday because of the courage and the spirit which you have brought to a dark period. Good luck to you.[19]

In the two pages of suggested speech text attached to his notes to Kennedy and Sorensen, Markel drafted the core ideas that Sorensen elaborated for the actual speech—the invocation of a cold war crisis, a justification for government secrecy, an appeal for greater foreign news coverage, and the request for voluntary press restraint, including the contrast between "Is it news?" and "Is it in the national interest?" Markel wrote, in part:

What are we required to do if now once more we are to achieve another victory in the struggle for freedom? We must recognize the dangers; we must be willing to sacrifice the soft life; we must meet our responsibilities.

As molders of public opinion, you can help greatly in this endeavor to alert the people to the peril and to urge them to meet the challenge. For a free press that is also responsible and that performs its primary task of information is vital to the survival of a democracy.

Let us not forget for a moment that a vast job of information confronts us—to clarify for the country and to the world our national purpose and our international intent.

This must be a joint enterprise of all the agencies of information—the mass media, the government, all the educational institutions. In this effort, the newspaper has a most important role because the printed word retains its power.

I need the help of the press. I am not asking you to support me on your editorial pages—this is not yet Utopia—but only that you do as much of the information assignment as you can in the news columns. There has been a notable advance in this direction and I applaud you for it. More power and presses to you.

Especially I urge you to print as much international news as you can, with as much explanation as possible, because in these areas especially understanding is needed. This is no longer foreign news—it is immediate, it is close to us—it is local news.

There is one sensitive area with which I feel I cannot fail to deal. In these days we must meet Communist methods with counter tactics—tactics that sometimes require a certain amount of so-called "classification." I am not criticizing you for what you have done; I am not suggesting censorship of any kind or an extension of classification. I am asking only that to the question: "Is it news?" you add the question: "Is it in the national interest?" For this is war, even though it is undeclared, and I believe profoundly that the same attitudes as in actual combat should and must guide us.

I have been told that editors and publishers sit in different pews and should be so segregated. But I believe in integration here, too, because yours is the ultimate responsibility.

I ask you, then, to join in this common crusade, for a better informed and thus a greatly strengthened nation.[20]

Although the tone of Markel's draft was in many ways unacceptable, its themes form the core of Sorensen's versions of the speech. Markel's joke about "integration" of editors and publishers was ill considered, but his assertion that the publishers had the "ultimate responsibility" to enforce press restraint, while oddly disloyal to his own role as an editor, became a key element of Kennedy's speech. Sorensen appears to have written two drafts of the speech—a "first draft" of eight pages and another draft of eleven pages. The files also contain a reading copy of the speech and the speech "as delivered," which contains some additional material apparently added by either Kennedy or Sorensen at the last minute.

It is clear from the revisions that the core message of the speech is a call for press restraint. The revisions and additions indicate, as well, an apparent attempt to cushion the predictably unwelcome message with ingratiation and humor. Kennedy begins the speech with an anecdote that appeared in none of the drafts, nor in the reading copy.

I appreciate very much your generous invitation to be here to-night.

You bear heavy responsibilities these days and an article I read some time ago reminded me of how particularly heavily the burdens of present day events bear upon your profession.

You may remember that in 1851 the New York *Herald Tribune,* under the sponsorship and publishing of Horace Greeley, employed as its London correspondent an obscure journalist by the name of Karl Marx.

We are told that foreign correspondent Marx, stone broke, and with a family ill and undernourished, constantly appealed to Greeley and Managing Editor Charles Dana for an increase in his munificent salary of $5 per installment, a salary which he and Engels ungratefully labeled as the "lousiest petty bourgeois cheating."

But when all his financial appeals were refused, Marx looked around for other means of livelihood and fame, eventually terminating his relationship with the *Tribune* and devoting his talents full time to the cause that would bequeath to the world the seeds of Leninism, Stalinism, revolution and the cold war.

If only this capitalistic New York newspaper had treated him more kindly; if only Marx had remained a foreign correspondent, history might have been different. And I hope all publishers will bear this lesson in mind next time they receive a poverty-stricken appeal for a small increase in the expense account from an obscure newspaper man.[21]

The anecdote about Karl Marx specifically asserts Kennedy's command of history—"an article I read some time ago"—and implicitly launches the theme that publishers have responsibilities over writers and editors. We know from the Schlesinger memo that Sorensen was aware that Kennedy was speaking not to the publishers themselves but to their advertising bureaus. But the rhetorically created audience was the publishers, and through them the editors and writers, all of whom are at several points dramatically cast as the objects of his direct address. The press is not "them" in this speech, it is "you," as when Kennedy says, "But I do ask every publisher, every editor, and every newsman in the nation to re-examine his own standards, and to recognize the nature of our country's peril." Later he says, "I am not asking your newspapers to support the Administration, but I am asking your help in the tremendous task of informing and alerting the American people." Markel had proposed:

> In these days we must meet Communist methods with counter tactics—tactics that sometimes require a certain amount of so-called "classification." I am not criticizing you for what you have done; I am not suggesting censorship of any kind or an extension of classification. I am asking only that to the question: "Is it news?" you add the question: "Is it in the national interest?" For this is war, even though it is undeclared, and I believe profoundly that the same attitudes as in actual combat should and must guide us.

Sorensen revised to achieve a less confrontational form that made a gesture unusual to this speech of reaching out to other constituencies, distinctly softening the directness of his key demand:

> Every newspaper now asks itself, with respect to every story: "Is it news?" All I suggest is that you add the question: "Is it in the interest of national security?" And I hope that every group in America— unions and businessmen and public officials at every level—will ask the same question of their endeavors, and subject their actions to this same exacting test.[22]

Kennedy's speech was bound to arouse some suspicion, at the very least, as to his intentions. He implicitly acknowledged this with a repeated series of denials and disavowals, a natural impulse given the sweeping but somewhat vague demand that the press consider its duty to the "national interest." The Salinger and Markel memos to Kennedy emphasized the adversarial positions of government and press. In their place, Kennedy and Sorensen put Kennedy on the side of the press, suggesting other, greater conflicts; he and the press were cast as against government censors, and, in a larger frame, as united in their conflict with the forces arrayed against the nation in the cold war. But the disavowals might backfire, drawing attention to themselves as an attempt to forestall criticism, as a trace of anticipated conflict between Kennedy and the press that he is working so energetically to dismiss. The effect is heightened by the repeated pairing of disavowals with "but" constructions, a pattern that might further arouse the suspicion that the real message comes after, not before, the "but." The disavowals are repeated in several contexts:

> I have selected as the title of my remarks tonight "The President and the Press." Some may suggest that this would be more naturally worded "The President Versus the Press." But these are not my sentiments tonight. . . .
>
> Nevertheless, my purpose here tonight is not to deliver the usual assault on the so-called one-party press. . . .
>
> Nor, finally, are these remarks intended to examine the proper degree of privacy which the press should allow to any President and his family. . . .
>
> The very word "secrecy" is repugnant in a free and open society; and we are as a people inherently and historically opposed to secret societies, to secret oaths and to secret proceedings. . . . And there is very grave danger that an announced need for increased security will be seized upon by those anxious to expand its meaning to the very limits of official censorship and concealment. That I do not intend to permit to the extent that it is in my control. And no official of my Administration, whether his rank is high or low, civilian or military, should interpret my words here tonight as an excuse to censor the news, to stifle dissent, to cover up our mistakes or to withhold from the press and the public the facts they deserve to know.

But I do ask every publisher, every editor, and every newsman in the nation to re-examine his own standards, and to recognize the nature of our country's peril. . . .

[Our adversary] conducts the Cold War . . . with a war-time discipline no democracy would ever hope or wish to match.

Nevertheless, every democracy recognizes the necessary restraints of national security—and the question remains whether those restraints need to be more strictly observed if we are to oppose this kind of attack as well as outright invasion.

For the facts of the matter are that this nation's foes have openly boasted of acquiring through our newspapers information they would otherwise hire agents to acquire through theft, bribery, or espionage. . . .

The newspapers which printed these stories were loyal, patriotic, responsible and well-meaning. Had we been engaged in open warfare they undoubtedly would not have published such items. . . . And my question tonight is whether additional tests should not now be adopted. . . .

That question is for you alone to answer. . . . But I would be failing in my duty to the Nation, in considering all of the responsibilities that we now bear and all of the means at hand to meet those responsibilities, if I did not commend this problem to your attention, and urge its thoughtful consideration. . . .

I have no intention of establishing a new Office of War Information to govern the flow of news. . . . But I am asking the members of the newspaper profession and the industry in this country to reexamine their own responsibilities, to consider the degree and the nature of the present danger, and to heed the duty of self-restraint which that danger imposes upon us all. . . .

I am not asking your newspapers to support the Administration, but I am asking your help in the tremendous task of informing and alerting the American people. . . .

I not only could not stifle controversy among your readers—I welcome it.

Kennedy's use of the "I am not . . . but I am . . ." structure and its several variations in the ANPA speech is repeated so often that it becomes virtually the primary structural feature of the address, calling attention to the issue of Kennedy's motives and casting Kennedy as anticipating that he is likely to be misunderstood. Sorensen and Kennedy had developed their celebrated balanced style over years of speechmaking, often using it to lend a sense of elevation and dignity to Kennedy's public speaking. All are familiar with the most notable instance, from the inaugural address: "And so, my fellow Americans: ask not what your country can do for you—ask what you can do for your country." In the ANPA speech, the balanced constructions are put to a different use, and though Sorensen and Kennedy here achieve a more dignified tone than the Salinger and Markel notes, their continued emphasis on Kennedy's motives preserves traces of the adversarial and defensive posture of those early drafts.

At least some members of the press were alert to Kennedy's language of identification in this period. In Kennedy's news conference of May 5, 1961, we find this passage:

Q. Mr. President, in the speech prepared for delivery in Chicago last Friday which you did not read [the White House had released an advanced text of the speech, but Kennedy delivered a different one], you said that the principal adversary was not the Russians but rather our own unwillingness to do what must be done. Could you clarify for us your thinking on that and indicate some field in which the American people have not done what their governmental leaders asked?

THE PRESIDENT. Well, the latter is not the correct—I said "our," not to make a distinction between the Government and the people. I was talking about the common problems of a free society.

I do wish that some of the speeches I give would get as much attention as the speeches which I do not give. [Laughter] . . .

Q. May I ask one followup question, sir? When you use the word "our," are you suggesting that it's the unwillingness of the Government and people to do what must be done?

THE PRESIDENT. I had not subjected that sentence to the— but what I do think is a problem is to, in a free society, to attempt to come to actions which permit us to compete successfully with the discipline of the Communist state. And I think it's probably not only true using the "our"—I would use it not only in the national sense, but also in the international sense.[23]

The timing of the speech also seems to have contributed to the suspicion with which it was received by the press. In one sense, it could be argued that the timing was highly appropriate, since the issues of freedom of information and press restraint had been rehearsed within the White House and aired in public at least since the beginning of the administration. Further, the specific timing of the speech, coming immediately after a failed invasion, lent support for Kennedy's claim that the cold war was a reality and that press leaks might have damaged the secrecy needed for success in the Cuban landings. But precisely those elements of timing could just as easily be turned against Kennedy on this occasion. Although it is true that the issues of freedom of information, news management, and press restraint had been in the air for months, the issues had not matured to the point that a presidential speech could hope to nudge a nearly resolved debate into consensus. The immediate situation was also unpromising. The failure at the Bay of Pigs had starkly raised the question of Kennedy's competence and maturity; though the press largely supported him, any apparent attempt by Kennedy to shift the blame for the failure was almost certain to run counter to the press themes most favorable to Kennedy—that he willingly took responsibility and had learned from the mistakes of the invasion. An attempt to limit press freedom during a week when some in the press were claiming that more vigorous press coverage of the preparations for the invasion might have headed off the disaster seems in retrospect ill timed, and likely to renew scrutiny of Kennedy's motives.

The difficulty that Kennedy described in his ANPA speech was widely regarded as real—"the dilemma faced by a free and open society in a cold and secret war." Kennedy was not alone in thinking the cold war a genuine challenge. In general terms, many in the press would have agreed with Kennedy that, "This deadly challenge imposes upon our society two requirements of direct concern both to the press and to the President—two requirements that may seem almost contradictory in tone, but which must be reconciled and fulfilled if we are to meet this national peril. I refer, first, to the need for greater public information; and, second, to the need for far greater official secrecy." And yet if common sense seems to indicate that Kennedy's speech was dangerously timed and riskily called attention to his own motives, a reading of press reactions reveals a somewhat more complex picture.

Some of the immediate press reaction to Kennedy's ANPA speech was negative; far from putting this portion of the press on the defensive, the speech aroused speculation about Kennedy's motives. *Newsweek* magazine reported that, "To his audience, the President's words instantly conveyed the strong smell of censorship." The press "could not help suspecting that behind the President's reasoning was a bitter irritation stemming from the debacle in Cuba and the contribution the press had made to that debacle."[24]

The narrative of attribution—that is, the story of President Kennedy's motives—was partly a creature of press defensiveness; partly a continuing deployment of the general narrative of presidential character, subjectivity, and motivation that we saw in the account of the ASNE speech and the early days of the Kennedy administration; partly a product of the speech itself, with its dominating frame of the speaker's intentions; and even, to some degree, an effect created by background press briefings before the speech.

The effect of a presidential speech is partly launched by the creation of expectations in background briefings to reporters. A story by Don Shannon, White House reporter for the *Los Angeles Times*, provides a clear example of this process. In his story printed on the day of the speech, hours before its delivery, Shannon gives an account of Kennedy's motives and intentions: "Mr. Kennedy, known to feel that the failure of the Cuba invasion attempt was due in part to the flood of advance news reports on the operation, is expected to appeal to publishers for restraint in dealing with national security affairs. He will be the principal speaker at the annual dinner of the Bureau of Advertising of the American Newspaper Publishers' Assn. at the Waldorf-Astoria."[25]

What John F. Kennedy was "known to feel" could thus be taken into account in a hard-news story about a speech that had not yet been delivered, but whose main points were also known.

In the days before and after the ANPA speech, the *Los Angeles Times* carried several stories about Kennedy's motives. A column by Republican Senator Barry Goldwater on April 27 speculated about Interior Secretary Udall's comment after the Cuban failure, quickly retracted, that the invasion had really been a creation of Eisenhower and Nixon, and was merely inherited by Kennedy. Goldwater used the occasion to speculate about Kennedy's motives and about the mechanics of behind-the-scenes government. In this account, Kennedy's real motives may be read not through his own words but through the words of his subordinates. "It is difficult for me to believe that President Kennedy would be a party to such a weasel attempt [as Udall's] to avoid responsibility for whatever part our government played in the Cuban fiasco.... It is equally difficult for me to believe that Mr. Udall would have offered his weak and unacceptable alibi, would have made such a reach in his attempt to avoid responsibility without first consulting the boss."[26]

Goldwater's story of Kennedy's character and motive is couched in the frame of Goldwater's character: his own decency prompts him to trust Kennedy, but his political savvy forces him to conclude that Udall would not have acted without Kennedy's deniable approval. As a political actor himself, Goldwater adds an ingredient not always present in press accounts of motive and mechanics—Goldwater is talking about political virtue, a subject that is also part of the Kennedy vocabulary.

An article by the *Los Angeles Times* Washington bureau chief, Robert Hartmann, later head of President Gerald Ford's speechwriting operation, also responded to the ANPA speech with an analysis of motive: "Now some cynics are saying that by laying it on the line in New York [at ANPA], President Kennedy has diverted the nation's newspapers from asking any more embarrassing questions about Cuba while they rally to defend their own freedom.... There are those in the President's official family capable of such political subtlety, but I choose to believe

Mr. Kennedy is sincerely grappling with the dilemma he put to the publishers. Can a free and open society discipline itself to compete with a closed and secret society in this strange kind of undeclared war?"[27]

In one of the few press references to speechwriting in reference to the ANPA speech, Hartmann concluded his article by using the possibility of ghostwriting to cast doubt on whether Kennedy actually wrote, or really believed in, his appeal to the press: "I still wonder which ghost wrote Mr. Kennedy's speech."[28]

In its news columns, the *Los Angeles Times* reported that the press supported Kennedy's call for press restraint. Don Shannon wrote on the day after the speech that, "A representative group of newspaper publishers and top executives of the nation's press expressed a willingness Thursday night to go along with President Kennedy's proposal for self-regulation of security by the nation's press."[29] But in the editorial pages, even when treating Kennedy with the most hostility, and with suspicion about his motives, the *Los Angeles Times* proclaimed its agreement with Kennedy's call for patriotic press restraint. *Times* editor Nick B. Williams angrily proclaimed that: "Two weeks in Washington and New York have convinced me that President John F. Kennedy doesn't care very much for American newspapers unless they are shouting his name with joyous hosannas.... But we do not intend to be browbeaten into sweeping under the rug any such horrible fiasco as the Cuban "invasion."... By all means let us have the secrecy that is essential to the nation's security. But let us not, at the same time, try to foist upon the press the blame for high-level government blabbering."[30]

The *Los Angeles Times* was a Nixon paper, and so perhaps its suspicion of Kennedy's call for press restraint was predictable. The *Boston Globe*, usually more sympathetic to Kennedy, ran page-wide headlines on the speech the morning after and reprinted most of the text. At the same time, the *Globe* respectfully debated his ANPA speech, while reading Kennedy's intentions between the lines: "Nowhere in his speech did the President specifically mention the recent Cuban fiasco, but it was clearly in his mind when he said that 'details of this nation's covert preparations to counter the enemy's covert operations have been available to every newspaper reader, friend and foe alike.'... It seems clear enough by now that the invasion failed not because of anything that was printed, but because of what was not printed and what the CIA should have found out and did not. The predicted mass uprising against Castro on which plans were based failed to occur. . . . Had the press been able to report accurately on Cuban sentiment, the stories might not, at the time, have been regarded by many as being 'in the national interest.' Yet in the light of hindsight, they could have avoided, later, a severe diplomatic setback for the United States."[31]

In another *Globe* story, James Marlow questioned "how much thinking Mr. Kennedy had done on the subject before suggesting self-censorship." Marlow argued that though Kennedy specifically denied any intention of imposing censorship on the press, a not-for-attribution administration news briefing "did in effect impose a limited kind of censorship." Marlow claimed that the news conference was not only censorship, but also that it was inept, and he traced the ineptitude directly to the issue of presidential identity and agency. At the off-the-record briefing, reporters were instructed not to name sources by name; they could, however, attribute what was said to "high officials" or "authoritative sources." "Thus," writes Marlow, "newspaper readers were deprived of full information." On the other hand, a reporter from the Polish Communist Party newspaper, *Tribuna Ludu,* was allowed into the briefing. "So, while American readers were left baffled about who said what, the Communist world was in a position to get a complete fill-in on everything said, with each speaker identified for the Communist bosses back home."[32]

Marlow's complaint, when read in the context of Kennedy's speech and the interpretive perspectives of other press accounts of the speech and the political context, provides an important challenge. In the Kennedy years, both the press and the politicians were working in the unfamiliar context of a cold war and in a rapidly changing communication environment. The presidency had become an increasingly rhetorical office under Theodore Roosevelt, Woodrow Wilson, Franklin Roosevelt, and now John F. Kennedy. As rhetorical power and drama expanded, so, too, did the practice of ghostwriting and the mechanics of government public relations. In its turn, the press, joined by radio and television, developed new practices and new idioms to cope with the flow of government information and, in some cases, to resist becoming its passive agents. In paradigm-shifting instances such as Robert Drew's film *Primary* and Theodore White's book *The Making of the President*, the public was invited to look behind the rhetoric at the backstage apparatus and the offstage actors. The daily press and weekly magazines embraced the new paradigms, meanwhile developing their own language of attribution—reporting not only what political leaders did and said, but also what they thought and meant.

At the same time that the mechanics of politics were becoming more professional, when political speeches were routinely written by one person and spoken by another, the media began to report politics in increasingly personal terms. These forces are all on display in the interaction of Kennedy and the press in April, 1961. Surely it was reasonable for the press and the nation to wonder if the failure of the Cuban invasion was evidence of an incompetent president, whether the president would accept responsibility, and whether the president would learn from the failure. Similarly, common sense seems to require that to understand a President's utterances, we need to know not only what he says but also to interpret what he means. But, of course, the press does not know what the President thinks or feels, and its unreflective assumption that it does blurs the already fuzzy line between reporting and interpretation, with consequences for both journalism and politics.

When James Marlow complained about the frustrations of reporting on an off-the-record administration briefing, he threw into sharp relief the near impossibility of making sense of "authoritative sources" if those sources could not be named and their identities used to assess their level of responsibility, their knowledge, their consistency, and their probable intentions.

The ASNE and ANPA speeches appear to have led to some direct action by both press and presidency. Both ANPA and the administration continued to consider issues of freedom of information, and Salinger organized a "publishers' luncheon" series starting in May, 1961, to bring about closer relations between Kennedy and the publishers through informal meetings.[33]

The Kennedy speeches of April, 1961, show how press attributions of presidential inner states—motives, thoughts, feelings—could be employed as a political resource or could backfire, and sometimes both at once. In the complex, competitive, and collaborative interaction of press and presidency, Kennedy and the administration used the resources of agency and anonymity even as the press used its counter-resources of attribution and analysis of motive to make sense out of an obscure and dangerous situation. The press appears to have emerged from the experience determined to be loyal but to retain its skepticism; the administration appears to have made some serious mistakes, and to have employed high-risk rhetoric to avert the impression of incompetence or lack of resolve.

The skepticism of the press is a precious national resource, but during the Kennedy administration we see it beginning to turn in a possibly self-defeating direction. The press naturally wants to avoid the restraints of an "objectivity" that, if observed rigidly, might require it to report on the staged events and rehearsed words of politicians as if they were "real" and not "pseudo" events, staged in order to be reported.[34] In its desire to tell more of the truth of public matters, the press in the 1960s developed a variety of journalistic rhetorics to get behind the scenes. But in getting behind the scenes, the press often, instead of doing the hard work of discovering the uncovered sources and effects of government policy, engaged in a rhetoric of attribution, adopting a narrative insinuating that it knew what the president was really thinking and feeling. The effects of a narrative of attribution can be paradoxical, since in narration, point of view—largely created by various means of suggesting the perspective of the central protagonist—shapes the audience's interest and sympathies. In this way, skeptical refusals to accept the façade may lead the press into a sort of gullibility about states of mind in the president they are portraying. Seeking skepticism, the press may, instead, actually enhance the effect of identification between president and public.

In supposing they knew what John F. Kennedy was thinking and feeling when he read a speech written by Theodore Sorensen, the press went too far, indulging in an implicit narrative of agency that had become so familiar it required no explicit support. Whereas the press was going too far in acting as the mediating agent with the gift of attributing inner states to the president, it found that the practice was met by two contrary administration tactics—direct address to the people and anonymous briefings for the press. The printed press complained in the early months of the Kennedy administration about live television presentation of full-length presidential press conferences, partly because the practice was claimed to change the quality of both questions and answers. The live press conference also deprived the printed press of important interpretive, mediating, and framing functions. In complaining about the difficulties of running a democracy by anonymous administrative briefings, the press again found itself unable to go far enough, because the practice denied the possibility of connecting the verbal act to its agent. In these ways, the competition between press and presidency in the Kennedy administration was to a considerable degree acted out in terms of the capacity of the president and the press to control not just the agenda, but also the characterization of the president's inner states and public competency.

This account of President John F. Kennedy's speeches to the American Society of Newspaper Editors and the American Newspaper Publisher's Association has emphasized the complex authorship of the speeches and has attempted to describe, and at the same time to avoid, even to disavow, the simultaneous magnification of Kennedy's persona and the routine attribution of interior states to that persona. At the same time, this account has adopted a perspective that does not presume to theorize away the capacity of John F. Kennedy to act as a historical agent. We have seen how Kennedy's speeches were fashioned by Theodore Sorensen with materials provided by agents of the government and members of the press, and how the texts of the speeches were filtered through press accounts. Both the speeches and the press accounts construct narratives of Kennedy's knowledge, intentions, and feelings. In all of this, John F. Kennedy may seem to be left as an empty shell. That would be a mistake. John F. Kennedy was, as he claimed to be, the "responsible officer of the government," not only an active but also the decisive figure in the drama, and by every account in command, even when mistaken. Kennedy the man was not, despite the complexity of the policy-making and the speech-making processes, a mere instrument of the system.

John F. Kennedy's interest in the curious relations of the press and the government did not begin with his presidency, or even with his entry into politics. More than twenty years before his election to the presidency, the young John Kennedy, in an honors thesis at Harvard University later published as *Why England Slept*, speculated on just these issues, sounding themes that he revisited in April, 1961. *Why England Slept*, first published in 1940 during the Battle of Britain, when it was by no means clear that England would survive the Nazi menace, begins with the question, "Why was England so poorly prepared for the war?" In this remarkably mature and prescient little book, Kennedy considers the complex and shared processes that led England to delay the rearmament that might have prepared it for a war that in retrospect seemed inevitable. Kennedy warned his readers that blaming England's situation on failed leadership was an inadequate explanation, and one that might mislead Americans at what had become a dangerous hour for the United States. Kennedy wrote that,

> Unlike Britain's leader, Stanley Baldwin, America's Roosevelt had been far ahead of public opinion in this country in his opposition to the dictatorship. Since his "Quarantine the aggressor" speech in 1937, he has introduced larger defense estimates than Congress was prepared to accept. In fact, his 1940 Naval appropriation was cut by over 500 million dollars not four months ago. I point this out as I wish to show that we should not dismiss England's position as being merely a question of lack of leadership. Our leadership has been outspoken, yet our positions still show a remarkable similarity.[35]

Kennedy argued that the responsibility for the failure to re-arm was shared by political leaders and the public, and that the press was a crucial force in shaping public opinion. As he was to do more than twenty years later in his speeches to the press, Kennedy considered the differences between the press systems in democracies and dictatorships. In comparing the systems of Nazi Germany with those of England and the United States, Kennedy observed that, "In a dictatorship, a vigorous armaments program can be carried on, even though the people are deeply hostile to the idea of going to war. The rigidly controlled state press can then build up a war psychology at any time."[36] Furthermore, "a democracy's free press gives the speeches of the totalitarian leaders, who state their case in such a 'reasonable' manner that it is hard always to see them as a menace," whereas dictatorships are able to exclude the speeches of democratic leaders.[37] In moments of crisis, "the dictator is able to know exactly how much the democracy is bluffing, because of the free press, radio, and so forth, and so can plan his moves accordingly."[38] But if the free press of the democracy gave a dictator short-run and tactical advantages, the long-run advantages were always with the democracy, since when it went to war it did so with the full support of its people, and since, "A great advantage that our free press should give us is an opportunity to recognize our own weaknesses as well as our own strength. In so recognizing them, we may be able to guard against them."[39]

And so when, on April 27, 1961, in his speech to the American Newspaper Publishers Association, Kennedy compared the press systems of the democracies with those of the dictatorships, he was returning to a theme to which he had given years of consideration. Oddly, Kennedy's long commitment to these ideas was obscured by the crisis of the moment—the very crisis that gave relevance to and motivated his ASNE and ANPA speeches. Kennedy's descriptions of the difficulties of a free press in time of international conflict could easily be portrayed—and were portrayed by some—as an opportunistic attempt to deflect criticism from himself and his administration and to blame the failure of the Bay of Pigs on the press.

And yet there is plenty of evidence for those who prefer the explanation that the ASNE and ANPA speeches were simply distractions, deflections—even deceptions. On the face of it, based on the speech texts themselves, the speeches dealt primarily with the press, and while they declared the importance of full information to preserve democracy, they provided little genuine information about the Cuban invasion. If we look at the effects of the speeches, insofar as they can be determined from the press coverage and Kennedy's steady support in opinion polls, whatever skepticism the press expressed about Kennedy's depiction of the press, he did manage to move the agenda and to sustain the view that a nation must support its president in time of crisis. Certainly Arthur Schlesinger thought the ANPA speech a mistake. Kennedy, he writes in *A Thousand Days,* "made his only misstep when . . . he told the press that it should be prepared to censor itself in the interests of national security. This went much too far, and he did not urge the point again."[40] Schlesinger describes a Kennedy trying to contain the damage, but not trying to deny it, to himself or to the public. On the day before the ANPA speech, Kennedy told Schlesinger, "We can't win them all. . . . And I have been close enough to disaster to realize that these things which seem world-shaking at one moment you can barely remember the next. We got a big kick in the leg—and we deserved it. But maybe we'll learn something from it."[41]

Kennedy might have won over some of his critics at the time of the ANPA speech had they been aware that his analysis of the press in time of conflict was not an overnight invention but a longstanding concern. On the other hand, had they known of the conversation later reported by Pierre Salinger, in which Salinger recalls that Kennedy criticized the press for damaging the chances of the Bay of Pigs operation, he might well have come off worse than he did. Of all the things that Kennedy wrote in *Why England Slept,* one brief passage may provide some perspective. "Every country makes great errors," Kennedy wrote, "and there is usually a good reason for it at the time."[42]

The complex interactions of speech making, speech writing, and the press continued through the Kennedy presidency and to the present. For Kennedy, suspicions of news management did not disappear, but neither did press fascination with John F. Kennedy. The crisis of April, 1961, marked by some floundering on both sides, prepared both Kennedy and the press for crises to come, especially in foreign policy and civil rights. But that's another story.

John F. Kennedy, Address "The President and the Press" before the American Newspaper Publishers Association, New York City, April 27, 1961

Mr. Chairman, ladies and gentlemen:

I appreciate very much your generous invitation to be here tonight.

You bear heavy responsibilities these days and an article I read some time ago reminded me of how particularly heavily the burdens of present day events bear upon your profession.

You may remember that in 1851 the New York *Herald Tribune*, under the sponsorship and publishing of Horace Greeley, employed as its London correspondent an obscure journalist by the name of Karl Marx.

We are told that foreign correspondent Marx, stone broke, and with a family ill and undernourished, constantly appealed to Greeley and Managing Editor Charles Dana for an increase in his munificent salary of $5 per installment, a salary which he and Engels ungratefully labeled as the "lousiest petty bourgeois cheating."

But when all his financial appeals were refused, Marx looked around for other means of livelihood and fame, eventually terminating his relationship with the *Tribune* and devoting his talents full time to the cause that would bequeath to the world the seeds of Leninism, Stalinism, revolution and the cold war.

If only this capitalistic New York newspaper had treated him more kindly; if only Marx had remained a foreign correspondent, history might have been different. And I hope all publishers will bear this lesson in mind the next time they receive a poverty-stricken appeal for a small increase in the expense account from an obscure newspaperman.

I have selected as the title of my remarks tonight "The President and the Press." Some may suggest that this would be more naturally worded "The President Versus the Press." But those are not my sentiments tonight.

It is true, however, that when a well-known diplomat from another country demanded recently that our State Department repudiate certain newspaper attacks on his colleague it was unnecessary for us to reply that this Administration was not responsible for the press, for the press had already made it clear that it was not responsible for this Administration.

Nevertheless, my purpose here tonight is not to deliver the usual assault on the so-called one-party press. On the contrary, in recent months I have rarely heard any complaints about political bias in the press except from a few Republicans. Nor is it my purpose tonight to discuss or defend the televising of Presidential press conferences. I think it is highly beneficial to have some 20,000,000 Americans regularly sit in on these conferences to observe, if I may say so, the incisive, the intelligent and the courteous qualities displayed by your Washington correspondents.

Nor, finally, are these remarks intended to examine the proper degree of privacy which the press should allow to any President and his family.

If in the last few months your White House reporters and photographers have been attending church services with regularity, that has surely done them no harm.

On the other hand, I realize that your staff and wire service photographers may be complaining that they do not enjoy the same green privileges at the local golf courses which they once did.

It is true that my predecessor did not object as I do to pictures of one's golfing skill in action. But neither on the other hand did he ever bean a Secret Service man.

My topic tonight is a more sober one of concern to publishers as well as editors.

I want to talk about our common responsibilities in the face of a common danger. The events of recent weeks may have helped to illuminate that challenge for some; but the dimensions of its threat have loomed large on the horizon for many years. Whatever our hopes may be for the future—for reducing this threat or living with it—there is no escaping either the gravity or the totality of its challenge to our survival and to our security—a challenge that confronts us in unaccustomed ways in every sphere of human activity.

This deadly challenge imposes upon our society two requirements of direct concern both to the press and to the President—two requirements that may seem almost contradictory in tone, but which must be reconciled and fulfilled if we are to meet this national peril. I refer, first, to the need for far greater public information; and, second, to the need for far greater official secrecy.

I.

The very word "secrecy" is repugnant in a free and open society; and we are as a people inherently and historically opposed to secret societies, to secret oaths and to secret proceedings. We decided long ago that the dangers of excessive and unwarranted concealment of pertinent facts far outweighed the dangers which are cited to justify it. Even today, there is little value in opposing the threat of a closed society by imitating its arbitrary restrictions. Even today, there is little value in insuring the survival of our nation if our traditions do not survive with it. And there is very grave danger that an announced need for increased security will be seized upon by those anxious to expand its meaning to the very limits of official censorship and concealment. That I do not intend to permit to the extent that it is in my control. And no official of my Administration, whether his rank is high or low, civilian or military, should interpret my words here tonight as an excuse to censor the news, to stifle dissent, to cover up our mistakes or to withhold from the press and the public the facts they deserve to know.

But I do ask every publisher, every editor, and every newsman in the nation to reexamine his own standards, and to recognize the nature of our country's peril. In time of war, the government and the press have customarily joined in an effort, based largely on self-discipline, to prevent unauthorized disclosures to the enemy. In time of "clear and present danger," the courts have held that even the privileged rights of the First Amendment must yield to the public's need for national security.

Today no war has been declared—and however fierce the struggle may be, it may never be declared in the traditional fashion. Our way of life is under attack. Those who make themselves our enemy are advancing around the globe. The survival of our friends is in danger. And yet no war has been declared, no borders have been crossed by marching troops, no missiles have been fired.

If the press is awaiting a declaration of war before it imposes the self-discipline of combat conditions, then I can only say that no war ever posed a greater threat to our security. If you are awaiting a finding of "clear and present danger," then I can only say that the danger has never been more clear and its presence has never been more imminent.

It requires a change in outlook, a change in tactics, a change in missions—by the government, by the people, by every businessman or labor leader, and by every newspaper. For we are opposed around the world by a monolithic and ruthless conspiracy that relies primarily on covert means for expanding its sphere of influence—on infiltration instead of invasion, on subversion instead of elections, on intimidation instead of free choice, on guerrillas by night instead of armies by day. It is a system which has conscripted vast human and material resources into the building of a tightly knit, highly efficient machine that combines military, diplomatic, intelligence, economic, scientific and political operations.

Its preparations are concealed, not published. Its mistakes are buried, not headlined. Its dissenters are silenced, not praised. No expenditure is questioned, no rumor is printed, no secret is revealed. It conducts the Cold War, in short, with a war-time discipline no democracy would ever hope or wish to match.

Nevertheless, every democracy recognizes the necessary restraints of national security—and the question remains whether those restraints need to be more strictly observed if we are to oppose this kind of attack as well as outright invasion.

For the facts of the matter are that this nation's foes have openly boasted of acquiring through our newspapers information they would otherwise hire agents to acquire through theft, bribery or espionage; that details of this nation's covert preparations to counter the enemy's covert operations have been available to every newspaper reader, friend and foe alike; that the size, the strength, the location and the nature of our forces and weapons, and our plans and strategy for their use, have all been pinpointed in the press and other news media to a degree sufficient to satisfy any foreign power; and that, in at least one case, the publication of details concerning a secret mechanism whereby satellites were followed required its alteration at the expense of considerable time and money.

The newspapers which printed these stories were loyal, patriotic, responsible and well-meaning. Had we been engaged in open warfare, they undoubtedly would not have published such items. But in the absence of open warfare, they recognized only the tests of journalism and not the tests of national security. And my question tonight is whether additional tests should not now be adopted.

That question is for you alone to answer. No public official should answer it for you. No governmental plan should impose its restraints against your will. But I would be failing in my duty to the Nation, in considering all of the responsibilities that we now bear and all of the means at hand to meet those responsibilities, if I did not commend this problem to your attention, and urge its thoughtful consideration.

On many earlier occasions, I have said—and your newspapers have constantly said—that these are times that appeal to every citizen's sense of sacrifice and self-discipline. They call out to every citizen to weigh his rights and comforts against his obligations to the common good. I cannot now believe that those citizens who serve in the newspaper business consider themselves exempt from that appeal.

I have no intention of establishing a new Office of War Information to govern the flow of news. I am not suggesting any new forms of censorship or new types of security classifications. I have no easy answer to the dilemma that I have posed, and would not seek to impose it if I had one. But I am asking the members of the newspaper profession and the industry in this country to reexamine their own responsibilities, to consider the degree and the nature of the present danger, and to heed the duty of self-restraint which that danger imposes upon us all.

Every newspaper now asks itself, with respect to every story: "Is it news?" All I suggest is that you add the question: "Is it in the interest of the national security?" And I hope that every group in America— unions and businessmen and public officials at every level—will ask the same question of their endeavors, and subject their actions to this same exacting test.

And should the press of America consider and recommend the voluntary assumption of specific new steps or machinery, I can assure you that we will cooperate whole-heartedly with those recommendations.

Perhaps there will be no recommendations. Perhaps there is no answer to the dilemma faced by a free and open society in a cold and secret war. In times of peace, any discussion of this subject, and any action that results, are both painful and without precedent. But this is a time of peace and peril which knows no precedent in history.

II.

It is the unprecedented nature of this challenge that also gives rise to your second obligation—an obligation which I share. And that is our obligation to inform and alert the American people—to make certain that they possess all the facts that they need, and understand them as well—the perils, the prospects, the purposes of our program and the choices that we face.

No President should fear public scrutiny of his program. For from that scrutiny comes understanding; and from that understanding comes support or opposition. And both are necessary. I am not asking your newspapers to support the Administration, but I am asking your help in the tremendous task of informing and alerting the American people. For I have complete confidence in the response and dedication of our citizens whenever they are fully informed.

I not only could not stifle controversy among your readers—I welcome it. This Administration intends to be candid about its errors; for, as a wise man once said: "An error doesn't become a mistake until you refuse to correct it." We intend to accept full responsibility for our errors; and we expect you to point them out when we miss them.

Without debate, without criticism, no Administration and no country can succeed—and no republic can survive. That is why the Athenian law-maker Solon decreed it a crime for any citizen to shrink from controversy. And that is why our press was protected by the First Amendment—the only business in America specifically protected by the Constitution—not primarily to amuse and entertain, not to emphasize the trivial and the sentimental, not to simply "give the public what it wants"—but to inform, to arouse, to reflect, to state our dangers and our opportunities, to indicate our crises and our choices, to lead, mold, educate and sometimes even anger public opinion.

This means greater coverage and analysis of international news—for it is no longer far away and foreign but close at hand and local. It means greater attention to improved understanding of the news as well as improved transmission. And it means, finally, that government at all levels, must meet its obligation to provide you with the fullest possible information outside the narrowest limits of national security—and we intend to do it.

III.

It was early in the Seventeenth Century that Francis Bacon remarked on three recent inventions already transforming the world: the compass, gunpowder and the printing press. Now the links between the nations first forged by the compass have made us all citizens of the world, the hopes and threats of one becoming the hopes and threats of us all. In that one world's efforts to live together, the evolution of gunpowder to its ultimate limit has warned mankind of the terrible consequences of failure.

And so it is to the printing press—to the recorder of man's deeds, the keeper of his conscience, the courier of his news—that we look for strength and assistance, confident that with your help man will be what he was born to be: free and independent.

Note: The president spoke at the annual dinner of the Association's Bureau of Advertising held at the Waldorf Astoria Hotel in New York City. His opening words "Mr. Chairman" referred to Palmer Hoyt, editor and publisher of the *Denver Post*, who acted as chairman of the dinner.

The text of the address is from *The Public Papers of the President* (1961).

John F. Kennedy, Off-the-Record Press Conference, "Backgrounder at State," April 25, 1961, State Department, Washington, D.C.

This document is a transcript that until 1997 was thought to have been lost. On July 8, 1997, the John F. Kennedy Library opened the document, which is a transcript of John F. Kennedy's half-hour, off-the-record meeting with the press on April 25, 1961. The meeting was held at the State Department. In the citation style of the present work, the document appears as: Transcript, JFK Backgrounder at State, April 25, 1961, "Presidential Backgrounder 4/25/61" Folder, Box 134, WH Staff Files, Pierre Salinger, John F. Kennedy Library. The document has apparently not previously been published in full, and although the briefing was referred to by the press in April, 1961, scholars have not previously had access to the document. The present author did not find it until April 21, 1999, after many attempts to track it down.

The document appears among the Salinger papers as a twenty-five-page typed transcript, with a heading written by hand at the top of the first page: "25 April 61—JFK Backgrounder at State." The pages are numbered with a numeral preceded by the letter "F," as in "F-1," "F-2," and so on. It is not known what the "F" stands for, though it may be an extension of the A–E series of presidential documents described in chapter 3, or it may be that, as the typescript in the Kennedy Library shows holes for a three-hole loose-leaf binder, the document was retained as section F of a notebook of other briefing materials. In the typescript, the questioner is represented by "Q" and President Kennedy by "THE PRESIDENT," though in part of the document "A" is substituted for "THE PRESIDENT." It is clear that Kennedy pursues in the background briefing many of the themes that appear in his speeches of the same week to the American Society of Newspaper Editors and the American Newspaper Publishers Association. The press, in its turn, questions him both about Cuba and about various issues related to press relations and news management. The complete text of the document follows.

25 April 61—JFK Backgrounder at State
5:00 P.M.

MR. TUBBY: I want to remind you that the President is appearing here and will speak on an off-the-record basis. The Secret Service informs me that if any of you have cameras with you you may take shots, but we don't want shots from your seats at the start of the conference.

PRESIDENT KENNEDY: Mr. Secretary, ladies and gentlemen, I am delighted that you have come to Washington, and I hope that your talks with members of the Government have been beneficial.

I do not have a speech. I will be glad to answer a few questions. That, perhaps, is the best way of bringing out those matters which are of interest to you.

Let me say, very briefly, that I think we move and live in an extremely perilous time.

I commented on Thursday, rather briefly, about the kinds of challenges which we face, the maldistribution of wealth in many countries of the world, the fact that so many millions, hundreds of millions of people in the southern half of the globe, live on the marginal edge of existence with a strong sense of ancient wrongs and grievances, which are exploited by our adversaries in each of these countries.

People who desire an improvement in their life are presented with the example of the Soviet Union—having come in the short time of 40 years from being a backward country of Europe into being first in space. The Soviet Union, and the Chinese example, of being able to mobilize all of the resources of the state for the service of the state, being able to mobilize all of their resources to permit an economic breakthrough—that, obviously, has great attractions to people who live on incomes of $50, $60, or $70 a year.

And when the Communists are successful, as they are in a case like Cuba, they then use all of the resources of the police state in order to eliminate resistance. Many are shot, others become refugees who might oppose; and then the apparatus is able to maintain itself under control.

In a sense, the Communists have to win only one election, and when people maybe get tired of the results and become disappointed that the Communists are able not to fulfill their promises, by then the police apparatus has gone to work with control of communications and all the rest, and they are able to maintain their power.

I would think that the United States and the Free World is, therefore, in for an extremely difficult decade.

Many of the countries of South America face extremely sharp social tensions within their borders. The Communists are extremely active, well-disciplined minorities. I do not accept the view that this is the wave of history, but they are able to exploit the social structure of those countries in order to seize control. The most obvious example, of course, is the case of Vietnam, where with only 15,000 guerrillas, or perhaps less, there is somewhat of a prospect that they may seize control of the country before many months are out; killing, as they have, 2,000 civil officers a year, and 2,000 police a year; attempting to win control by assassination, even though the President has been re-elected by a generous margin. So I think we are in for a serious struggle.

In addition, of course, the Soviet Union and the United States are rather in balance as far as nuclear weapons goes, both having the ability to destroy each other; and, therefore, there is a reluctance on both sides to use those weapons. But, in conventional forces, the Soviet Union operating from a narrow base, the hub of the wheel, and the Communist Chinese in Asia outnumber us. They are able to bring far more troops to bear in the Middle East (the Russians are) than we are; and in Western Europe, with a long line of communication, far more troops than we can bring to bear; in Asia, through the Communist Chinese, they have them by the hundreds of thousands, and they can bring far more to bear than we can. And, therefore, with only the United States really in a position to move troops from one area to another, they have many advantages. And seconding the conventional force, of course, is their effective use of guerrillas. They are able to operate anonymously. Everything we do is printed in the paper; and they are carrying on their struggles with all of the advantage of secrecy.

I do not accept the view that there is a slow inevitability about the defeat of the West. I hold a different view. But I do not think I exaggerate when I say that we are going to be in for extremely difficult times which will test our nerve and will, because I think the Soviet Union will face us with the challenges in the most abrupt ways in the coming months: Berlin, Latin America, the Middle East, Asia, as they begin to continue to try to move the balance of power in their direction.

So that I am glad that you are here, because I feel that, being here, you can at least share some of the problems that we face, and with which we must deal in the coming months.

I will be delighted to answer any questions.

Q Mr. President, one of the things we have been told here is that a result of the events in Cuba has been to reveal to many other Latin American countries, governments, and peoples, Castro as a Communist stooge; and, therefore, to consolidate Latin American association with the United States.

Would you comment on that view?

THE PRESIDENT: I think that it is becoming—that many more people in Latin America are becoming more and more aware of the fact that the Cuban revolution is not an endemic one, or, if it was, that it has been taken over and is part now of the Soviet apparatus. Castro still has, of course, strong areas of support in many of the countries of Latin America. And I think it would be premature to make a judgment as to whether the awareness of the fact that Castro has betrayed the revolution—whether that awareness is moving faster than his popularity because of his association with the overthrow of existing social orders, which, in many cases, in Latin America are unpopular.

So that I think only time will tell which will win that race. But I would say that Castro as part of the Soviet apparatus—that that recognition is becoming greater. Many leaders of Latin America tell us that, but they are reluctant to say it publicly because of the support that Castro has in their own country.[1]

Q Mr. President, how badly damaged do you think United States prestige abroad has been, as a result of our involvement in the abortive Cuban invasion attempt, and what can we do to restore it to its previous state?

THE PRESIDENT: Well, I think the prestige of the United States has been hurt because a failure hurts. As to what we can do to restore it, that's a matter which we are considering. But I think that we are going to have to recognize that in these next years there are going to be many setbacks, and I hope many successes.

But in this struggle, which, after all, we are seeing a similar kind of struggle being carried on by the communists in Viet Nam—but that kind of support of guerrillas is not regarded—which is far more brutal, and directed as I have said to eliminating important groups within the society—that does not seem to be regarded very critically in the United Nations and elsewhere. But we will have to—I think our prestige, our survival are all at stake, and will be for the next ten years.

I know of no sure formula for success. All we can attempt to do is try to secure the best judgments of the people who have the most experience, and try, and if we fail, then we are going to try again.

Q Mr. President—

THE PRESIDENT: Perhaps in a different way, however, next time.

Q Mr. President, the argument has been made that the very strength of the reporting on the preparations for the Cuban invasion indicated how much leakage and how much faction-ridden this operation was, and it should have been a warning that it was an ill-founded one.

On the other hand, the argument was made that the press did a disservice by the extent of its reporting. Have you given any thought to what is the role of the press in covering para-military warfare?

THE PRESIDENT: Well, I hope the press will consider it. It's very difficult for a public official to discuss this matter, because it is a sensitive matter.

The press is rightfully concerned with any efforts to limit its reporting of events. The press, however, is a Fourth Estate, and therefore in a sense has important public responsibilities. It seems to me that it's a matter which the press should consider.

I think, if you go over the reports which have been made in recent weeks—many of them inaccurate—many of the reports coming out of Miami were inaccurate. Others were accurate, coming out of different areas, and which were extremely damaging to us.

If we were attempting to carry on any other operations in this or other areas, the next day, or even once we made a decision, undoubtedly it would be printed in the paper. And any preparations which were made would be printed in the paper.

One paper did carry a very carefully detailed analysis of the business about the defecting pilots, as to how the story couldn't possibly be true, one, two, three, four, at a time when we were under attack at the United Nations.

Now, this is a matter that you gentlemen have to decide in this kind of a cold war, what you should print and what you should not print.

I, of course, have thoughts about it. But I must say it seems to me that this is an area where you ought to make your judgments, and perhaps consider it almost as a profession, not merely individually. Because we are going to have, I hope, not a similar situation, but other situations which will require us to complete any preparations we make, and before we carry them on, and you reporters can always determine what is going on here.

Q Mr. President, if you had the Cuban decision to make over again, what would you have done differently? [Laughter]

THE PRESIDENT: Well, we hope that by the time General Taylor can conclude his analysis—I will say that, speaking here privately, many meetings were held on this matter.

Many people—whose experience had carried them through many years—judgments were reached, in both military and other branches of the Government. And this was not—when the decision was made, those who were most involved thought that this effort would be worthwhile, on the assumption that if it did not succeed there, that they could carry on as guerrillas.

But it failed. So quite obviously, with the advantage of hindsight, a good many different decisions would have been made. But I must say that a good many able people, with long military experience and all the rest, looked at this, and were wrong.

Q Mr. President, does the Administration still have under consideration an embargo on the sixty or seventy million dollars a year of imports from Cuba?

THE PRESIDENT: That's correct. But you have to realize that this is not going to make much difference. He can get along without that. It's sort of a gesture, and may be useful, worth doing. But it doesn't do the job, in any sense.

Q Mr. President, do you feel you have gained popular support for your foreign policy through your recent visits with Nixon, Rockefeller, and Eisenhower?

THE PRESIDENT: No. But I think they are entitled, as leaders of the—and as people who have strong support in the country, that they are entitled to be informed about events. And in addition it seems to me useful for me to get their views on what future action should be taken. And I have been doing that.

Q Mr. President, you said earlier that Viet-Nam is in danger and the Communists may win there in a few months.[2]

A Well, the argument has been made they may. We don't know what is going to happen in Viet-Nam.

Q Don't you think it is inevitable?

A No, I don't. But I certainly say that Viet-Nam is under very hard attack. If you look at a map of Viet-Nam under what areas the Communists control at night, the map is, there's a lot of red on it. So that I would say that that is a crucial area right now and these Communists supply from across the Southern border under the direction of the

Communists, are carrying out a very sharp and continual attack upon Viet-Nam and on the structural government. So I think it's a very critical area.

Q But not an effort we lost?

A No, I didn't suggest that. I think it's going to be a tough fight though in Viet-Nam.

Q Mr. President, do you have any information on who is training the Castro militia? Are there Soviet military experts there working with them, or guiding them on policy?

A Well, there is—I think it would be too, our information is harder. I think it would be better to pass it, the question. We are not making any assumptions any more. [Laughter] [Applause]

Q Mr. President, while Mr. Stevenson spoke here, he expressed the fear that in reference to American dollars being used overseas, that the use of corporate and private dollars investments overseas might be interpreted as a new form of colonialism. Is this a policy of your Administration?

A No. We are attempting in some areas to encourage private investments by giving reinsurance guarantees and all the rest. For example, on the development of the Volta, we are attempting to persuade private companies to come in and giving them some assurances that their risks will be at least borne in part by us.

So I would say that we wish to encourage investment. And I do think that, of course, those who invest in those countries must recognize that they are always going to be subject to the charge of exploitation and, therefore, they should take [e]very effort that they can by permitting local participation, local employees holding high and responsible positions, making sure that the pay is better than it may be in other sections, making sure that they don't dominate a particular industry which would be regarded as essential to the national security because whatever investment we carry in the mood that these countries are now in, where they have thrown off political domination from abroad, many of them are Marxists and regard economic exploitation as the modern form of colonialism, and therefore we have to constantly be on the alert against that charge, and the companies involved must be.

But I would like to see as within the limitations that I have described, I would hope that we would get more private investment particularly in the underdeveloped world and not merely in the extracted industries—oil, and so on.

Q We are always hearing, Mr. President, that we shall meet our bigger threats and tests in the next few years. Now, this implies that if we survive these tests and threats the threats will lessen. What is the basis for this assumption, and what is the long-range expectation along those lines of the Administration?

A Well, it is felt that this is a particularly critical time because these countries are going through a period of transition, particularly in Africa, from a colonial status into an independent status and therefore they now are attempting to make that adjustment. If they are able to make that adjustment and begin to build a stronger social structure within their country, if they begin to develop economic plans which offer them some hope of a gradually increasing standard of living over a period of years, they may be able to move through this particular period.

It may be unfair, I suppose it's just a tendency to think of the next few years. I think we are going to find ourselves confronted with great difficulties when the Chinese Communists secure the atomic weapons and, operating behind that cover, attempt to use the power of their conventional forces.

So that I would say the whole decade is critical and that is about as far as we can now look. But at least the plus side is the fact that these countries—India, Pakistan, and others—have laid out economic plans which do give some hope that at the end of them they will have made a breakthrough and they will begin gradually building sufficient capital to permit them, even in spite of their population increases, to provide for a better standard of living for their people. But I think probably we would be safe to say that even when that time comes other hazards will be upon us and as long as this struggle goes on between these powerful systems, the Communists and ours, I would say that life would be hazardous.

Q Mr. President?

A Yes?

Q Sir, from what you said about our being so badly out-numbered in Asia and from your reference to use of—I think you meant the Monroe doctrine before the editors, should we look forward to a return to a sphere of influence and a sphere of interests defense rather than world wide?

A No, I would not be prepared to accept that. I think that we can give guarantees to countries which can be maintained against external attack of the movement of foreign troops in the traditional sense across a frontier. That we can help them. We can, of course, deadlock the Communists' atomic power. But it's pretty hard to protect a country against the internal insurrections and guerrilla warfare and all the rest.

We can give them supplies. We can give them economic aid and all the rest, but in the final analysis they have to do that job. We cannot hold a country against internal attack, which is the kind of attack as the Communists—Khrushchev made it very clear in his speech in January—the war of the liberation and all the rest, that they are going to mount against us, feeling that when we then intervene they will threaten us with an atomic war or will attack another country with conventional forces.

So that the problem is how do you hold these countries, not against external attack which I think we can meet our commitments to do, but internal. I think that is the problem. We see it in Laos. We see it in Viet-Nam. We are going to see it in other areas.

We can protect. I doubt if the Russians or the Chinese would move their troops formally across the frontier unless it was in reprisal to some action that we took. I think the threat of war with the United States is sufficient to prevent that. But inside the country in the final analysis we can help, but the people themselves have to win that fight. And it's extremely difficult for a society in those countries, which is not organized and not subject to the discipline which the Communists are, to win that fight. But that is the kind of fight we are going to have, and we are going to have it in this Hemisphere too.

Q Mr. President, I have a question about the space program. Yesterday we were told that we might have some equality with the Russians in 1967 to 1970 if we are willing to go all out in our financial support. Now, it seemed to me that we were told that this had to come from the people. Now, I come from the Mid-West and in my part of the country the people are very alarmed about Russia's advantage in the space program. Is there a tendency to wait for the people to come and say that we have to spend more money, or are there plans to go ahead with it as fast as possible no matter what the cost? And also to what extent is our military standing affected by the success of the space program?[3]

THE PRESIDENT: Well, I think I agree, and in a question as sophisticated as this one is the direction should come from here, not from the people. We should attempt to suggest what we think ought to be done, and the people can accept it or not. I will say it is an extremely difficult decision, as I am sure you have been informed, as we are talking about billions of dollars, and where there is no assurances that even if we put the billions of dollars in that we can be successful, at least in the sense of being first. We are behind in boosters by quite a lot. They obviously are not going to give away that advantage, and they are going to use the concentrated resources of their state to stay ahead.

So when we talk, we are talking about putting a man in the moon and bringing him back, we are talking, as you have been informed, about a program between 20 or 30 billion dollars with no assurance that in '69 or '70, or when it comes about, that we will be the first. We may be second by a week or a month, and we would have spent this tremendous sum of money and committed it to a program which does not have immediate military significance, which does not effect—it has a military significance, but being—it may not have the most extreme military significance. There may be other things that you would want to do militarily which do not involve a trip to the moon and back. Though I think that the whole question of space, we don't know what it is going to mean militarily. It is like the old quotation, "What good is a baby?" The question is, "What is the baby going to become?" And it is true about space. We don't know what it is going to be. It may be a decisive military aid. In any case we are talking about committing between 20 and 40 billion dollars to bring a man to the moon and back but with no assurance that we will be first. We are talking about another many billions of dollars and the way of putting a laboratory around the earth with two or three men, or to send a probe to the moon, around it, the moon and back, which could be done in a shorter time, but we are talking about a tremendous sum of money, and I do—the Vice President, who is Chairman of the Space Council now is conducting a study of this and is going to make recommendations, I would hope, in the next two or three weeks, which will then be the basis for a report to the Congress as to where we stand and what our alternatives are, and what our prospects are for success. But there as yet we have not been informed by a scientist that we are sure of being successful. But it may still be worth taking the risk, but it is a tremendous sum of money, and the Middle West and the rest of the country have to realize that we are talking about billions. When we are talking about putting four million dollars into desalinization and we are talking about other programs, oceanography and all the rest, we are talking now about the billions and billions of dollars, as I say, up to 40 billions, and that is a tremendous sum.

Q Mr. President, we have heard in the past few days a considerable explanation of the bad position that we face and the problems that we face. You have of course tapped it with your own discussion.[4] Is there any area that you see where at the present time, of dealing with Khrushchev and the rest of the Communist world, where we have some advantages and something constructive and hopeful to look forward to in terms of the Western world?

THE PRESIDENT: Well, I think we have many advantages. I think the potential of Western Europe is an extremely important one. After all, there are more people than there are in the Soviet Union, a greater productive capacity, and while there are serious problems in Western Europe, nevertheless that does offer a great hope for more intimate association between Western Europe and the United States.

The Communists have not taken control of any country in the Hemisphere and there are powerful groups opposed to the Communists, and Japan has moved ahead and in a far more prosperous way than we imagined some years ago. I do have great hopes that in spite of the problems that they face, India, which contains within its borders 35 to

40 per cent of all the peoples of the underdeveloped world, that they would be able in a third five-year plan to move ahead. I think it is clear that there is hope that they will continue to maintain their opposition to Communist advance within their own country.

So I would say that we have got tremendous disadvantages in this struggle, when you look at Africa, and the history of Africa, and the illiteracy, and the fact that they have been exploited, they feel, by the West, and they have suddenly become independent, and yet at the present time not one of them have as yet become, even though Mali and Guinea have become critical areas, at least they are still not Communist, nor any of the countries of Latin America, nor any of the countries of Western Europe.

There are also strong pressures within the Communist system itself, between Russia and China, and between the satellite countries and the Soviet Union.

So I just—I am conscious of our problems, but I think we sometimes ignore the fact that people really desire to be their own masters, that nations desire to be their own masters. I would say even in Guinea, which is probably the closest to the Communist orbit of any, that Sekou Touré does not desire to be a Communist puppet. He feels that he can develop his country. He is a Marxist. But there is a strong national feeling. Even the relations between China and Russia show it. So that all that serves, because these people's desire to be independent serves us. I think—I am conscious of our problems, but I think it is appropriate to point out that we have opportunities too.

Q Mr. President?

THE PRESIDENT: Yes.

Q In view of the situation in Berlin, maybe—are we possibly misjudging our comparative strengths, ours and the Russians, by the fact that Khrushchev seems to be dodging that situation? That is the one place where we are absolutely committed. Would you comment on that please?

THE PRESIDENT: Well, I think that there is some chance that we are going to have an encounter about Berlin, and there is no indication that he is going to postpone it indefinitely. His letter to Adenauer in February indicated his desire to come back to the question of Berlin. I have no doubt that that is going to be brought to our attention very prominently in a couple of months, and it is an area where of course we have strategic problems, but it is an area where we are clearly committed. So I would say that I think that is going to be a test of our nerves today. I don't think it is fair to say he is dodging it. I think he is heading toward it.

Q Mr. President, we seem to have heard nothing but sad news the last few days. I wondered—I am from Kentucky—if you would care to comment on the Kentucky Derby next month?

[laughter]

THE PRESIDENT: That is going to be sad for everybody who loses, too. [Laughter] But there are more losers than winners. Now, on the other hand, the news from Algeria this afternoon is encouraging. So I don't want you to come down here and get put through the wringer and feel that everybody in Washington is—I just think that these problems require the best judgment of all of us, and I suppose, to know where we are going we must know where we have been, and I think that there is a good deal of soul searching now going on in this Administration, which I think is a good thing.

Q Mr. President, has there ever been any consideration given to the establishment of a police force under the Organization of the American States to meet this problem in Latin America?

THE PRESIDENT: Yes, and it is one of the matters that we have been considering now. In the past however there has not been sufficient commitment to it by any. This and other proposals are now being considered now [sic]. Perhaps we can have one more, and then I shall go.

Q Mr. President, in the earlier considerations in this conference, the failure of the Cuban operation or the failure of the intelligence, both militarily and in terms of Castro's, the man who makes the intelligence in his backgrounder denies this and implies it was more a question of the failure of military tactics. I wonder if you can give us your ideas on this.

THE PRESIDENT: Well, I think it is most unwise to make any judgments about it now, and that is the reason that General Taylor, one of the reasons why General Taylor is pursuing this entire matter, not to attempt to find out who is wrong, because a good many people were wrong, but to find out how they could have been wrong and what we can do in the future to improve any relationship between intelligence and military operations and decisions. So I'm not familiar with what was said, but I would reserve judgment on the question of failures, because I think that we are going to know a good deal more about it. I have my own opinion, but I don't think that there is any use in saying what was wrong was the military or what was wrong was the intelligence. I think that maybe everybody has a piece of this. [laughter]

Q Mr. President, now that you have been in office for three months, how do you like it?

THE PRESIDENT: Well, I liked it better up to about nine days ago. [Laughter; applause]

MR. TUBBY: This is off the record, what the President said. At the beginning I said that and I want to reiterate everything that he said now was off the record.

[Whereupon, at 5:31, the meeting was concluded.]

Notes

Chapter 1

1. Jeffrey K. Tulis, *The Rhetorical Presidency*. The Tulis formulation remains controversial—and productive—among political scientists and rhetoricians. For the main lines of analysis, see especially Martin J. Medhurst, ed., *Beyond the Rhetorical Presidency*; Richard J. Ellis, ed., *Speaking to the People*; Kathryn M. Olson, "Rhetoric and the American President," *The Review of Communication* 1 (2001): 247–53. For the original formulation of the doctrine see James W. Ceaser, Glen E. Thurow, Jeffrey Tulis, and Joseph M. Bessette, "The Rise of the Rhetorical Presidency," in *Rethinking the Presidency*, ed. Thomas E. Cronin (Boston: Little, Brown, 1982).

2. Montague Kern, Patricia W. Levering, and Ralph B. Levering, *The Kennedy Crises: The Press, the President, and Foreign Policy*, xii.

3. Kern, Levering, and Levering, *The Kennedy Crises*, 3.

4. Ibid., xii.

5. Steven R. Goldzwig and George N. Dionisopoulos, *"In a Perilous Hour": The Public Address of John F. Kennedy*; Vito N. Silvestri, *Becoming JFK: A Profile in Communication*; Kimber Charles Pearce, *Rostow, Kennedy, and the Rhetoric of Foreign Aid*; and Garth E. Pauley, *The Modern Presidency and Civil Rights: Rhetoric on Race from Roosevelt to Nixon*.

6. Theodore J. Lowi, *The Personal President: Power Invested, Promise Unfulfilled*, 9. See Richard E. Neustadt, *Presidential Power and the Modern Presidents: The Politics of Leadership from Roosevelt to Reagan*.

Chapter 2

1. Aristotle, *On Rhetoric*, trans. George A. Kennedy (New York: Oxford University Press, 1991), 38. The brackets in the quoted passage are from Kennedy.

2. See, for example, Edwin Black, "The Second Persona," *Quarterly Journal of Speech* 56 (1970): 109–19; Maurice Charland, "Constitutive Rhetoric: The Case of the *Peuple Quebecois*," *Quarterly Journal of Speech* 73 (1987): 133–50; Walter J. Ong, "The Writer's Audience Is Always a Fiction," in *Interfaces of the Word* (Ithaca, N.Y.: Cornell University Press, 1977), 53–81; Thomas W. Benson, "Rhetoric as a Way of Being," in *American Rhetoric: Context and Criticism*, ed. Thomas W. Benson (Carbondale: Southern Illinois University Press, 1989), 293–322.

3. Thomas E. Patterson, *Out of Order*, 7–8. In this passage, Patterson footnotes Michael Robinson, "Improving Election Information in the Media" (Paper presented at the Voting for Democracy Forum, Washington, D.C., September 11, 1983), 2.

4. Patterson, *Out of Order*, 19.

5. Ibid., 245.

6. Ibid., 69, 71.

7. Deborah Mathis, "Public Press, Private Lives," in response to a question after a talk at the Shorenstein Center on the Press, Politics, and Public Policy, John F. Kennedy School of Government, Harvard University, February 16, 1999.

8. Robert Drew, Richard Leacock, and Donn Pennebaker, *Primary* (1960), Motion Picture.

9. Theodore H. White, *The Making of the President, 1960;* see also Norman Mailer, *Miami and the Siege of Chicago;* Joe McGinniss, *The Selling of the President, 1968;* Timothy Crouse, *The Boys on the Bus;* Richard Ben Cramer, *What It Takes: The Way to the White House;* Thomas W. Benson, "Another Shooting in Cowtown," *Quarterly Journal of Speech* 67 (1981): 347–406. The rhetorical resources for reporting "behind the scenes" and bringing a literary sensibility to the literature of fact had a long development before the 1960s; see, for example, Henry Mayhew, *London Labour and the London Poor;* George Orwell, *Down and out in Paris and London;* James Agee and Walker Evans, *Let Us Now Praise Famous Men;* Lillian Ross, *Picture.*

10. Joseph W. Alsop, Jr., *Reporting Politics,* the Fourteenth Annual Memorial Lecture sponsored by the Twin Cities Local, American Newspaper Guild, AFL-CIO, and the School of Journalism, University of Minnesota, Minne-

apolis, October 17, 1960 (Minneapolis, Minn.: American Newspaper Guild, 1960), 9.

11. Alsop, *Reporting Politics*, 5.

12. John Fischer, *Magazine and Newspaper Journalism: A Comparison*, The Sixteenth Annual Memorial Lecture sponsored by the Twin Cities Local, American Newspaper Guild, AFL-CIO, and the School of Journalism, University of Minnesota, Minneapolis, October 11, 1962 (Minneapolis, Minn.: American Newspaper Guild, 1962), n.p.

13. For general accounts, see James Aronson, *The Press and the Cold War;* Joseph P. Berry, Jr., *John F. Kennedy and the Media: The First Television President;* Worth Bingham and Ward S. Just, "The President and the Press," *Reporter,* April 12, 1962, 18–23; Michael Baruch Grossman and Martha Joynt Kumar, *Portraying the President: The White House and the News Media;* Montague Kern, Patricia W. Levering, and Ralph B. Levering, *The Kennedy Crises: The Press, the Presidency, and Foreign Policy;* Louis Liebovich, *The Press and the Modern Presidency: Myths and Mindsets from Kennedy to Clinton;* James E. Pollard, "The Kennedy Administration and the Press," *Journalism Quarterly* 41 (1964): 3–14; Pierre Salinger, *With Kennedy;* Harry Sharp, Jr., "Live from Washington: The Telecasting of President Kennedy's News Conferences," *Journal of Broadcasting and Electronic Media* 13 (1968): 23–32; John Tebbel and Sarah Miles Watts, *The Press and the Presidency: From George Washington to Ronald Reagan.*

14. "The Races," *Boston Globe*, April 16, 1961, 44; the same UPI telephoto was printed in the *Washington Post.*

15. *Boston Globe*, April 16, 1961, 3.

16. "Luncheon at the White House," *Boston Globe*, April 12, 1961, 47.

17. "JFK: Report #2," NBC White Paper, NBC News, April 11, 1961.

18. Doris Fleeson, "Lunch with the President's Wife," *Boston Globe*, April 13, 1961, 12.

19. "Anxious Mrs. Kennedy to Fight for Children's Right of Privacy," *Boston Globe*, April 12, 1961, 1. The story includes a photograph of Caroline Kennedy.

20. Kate Lang, "Revolution in the White House III: No Longer the Look of a Harvard Soph," *Boston Globe*, April 25, 1961, 14.

21. "A Worried President Kennedy Will Confer with Former President Eisenhower Today," *Boston Globe,* April 22, 1961, 5, UPI Telephoto.

22. "Before and After," *Boston Globe,* April 29, 1961, 1.

23. "Guarded Grins, Unguarded Gloom," *Newsweek,* May 8, 1961, 24. The same two photographs were printed in the *Boston Globe* on April 26, with headline, "Take Your Choice"; in the "gloom" photograph we are told that they are "caught in a grim mood" after a breakfast discussion with the president on "world crises," *Boston Globe,* April 26, 1961, 1.

24. "Thoughtful," *Los Angeles Times,* April 20, 1961, 1, AP Wirephoto.

25. Alan L. Otten, "What Do You Think, Ted?" in *The Kennedy Circle,* ed. Lester Tanzer (Washington, D.C.: Luce, 1961), 7.

26. Otten, "What Do You Think, Ted?" 7.

27. Theodore C. Sorensen, conversation with the author, Cambridge, Mass., March 9, 1999.

28. Memo, "Possible Speech Topics for ASNE—April 20—and Publishers Bureau of Advertising—April 27," n.d., "American Newspaper Publishers Association, 4/27/61, Draft & Memoranda, 4/7/61–5/2/61 & undated" folder, Box 60, Theodore C. Sorensen Papers, JFK Speech Files 1961–63, John F. Kennedy Library (hereafter JFKL).

29. Speech draft, n.d., "Address before the American Society of Newspaper Editors 4/20/61" folder, Box 34, President's Office Files, Speech Files, JFKL.

30. Speech draft, "Introductory Material for ASNE Speech," n.d., "American Society of Newspaper Editors 4/20/61 Drafts & Press Release, 4/20/61 & Undated" folder, Box 60, Theodore C. Sorensen Papers, JFK Speech Files 1961–63, JFKL. An earlier, handwritten draft of the introductory material, titled "Introductory Material (Separate)" is also found in the ASNE folder in Box 60 of the Sorensen JFK speech files.

31. Speech draft, "1st Draft," n.d., "American Society of Newspaper Editors 4/20/61 Drafts & Press Release, 4/20/61 & Undated" folder, Box 60, Theodore C. Sorensen Papers, JFK Speech Files 1961–63, JFKL. The draft is on lined, yellow legal paper, handwritten.

32. Speech draft, "ASNE SPEECH," n.d., "American Society of Newspaper Editors 4/20/61 Drafts & Press Release, 4/20/61 & Undated" folder, Box 60, Theodore C. Sorensen Papers, JFK Speech Files 1961–63, JFKL. Typed draft, 3 pages.

33. Speech draft, American Society of Newspaper Editors, "American Society of Newspaper Editors 4/20/61 Drafts & Press Release, 4/20/61 & Undated" folder, Box 60, Theodore C. Sorensen Papers, JFK Speech Files 1961–63, JFKL. On this draft, there is a handwritten insert page after page 2, another handwritten insert page after page 3, and a new, typed page 4.

34. Speech draft, "Undated 2nd draft," "American Society of Newspaper Editors 4/20/61 Drafts & Press Release, 4/20/61 & Undated" folder, Box 60, Theodore C. Sorensen Papers, JFK Speech Files 1961–63, JFKL.

35. Speech draft, "3rd draft, ASNE Speech, 4/20/61," "American Society of Newspaper Editors 4/20/61 Drafts & Press Release, 4/20/61 & Undated" folder, Box 60, Theodore C. Sorensen Papers, JFK Speech Files 1961–63, JFKL. In the upper left-hand corner of this draft is the notation "2 p.m.," referring not to the time of the draft but to the time at which the speech is to be delivered on April 20.

36. Speech text, for release at 2:00 P.M., April 20, 1961, "American Society of Newspaper Editors 4/20/61 Drafts & Press Release, 4/20/61 & Undated" folder, Box 60, Theodore C. Sorensen Papers, JFK Speech Files 1961–63, JFKL.

37. President's Reading Copy, "American Society of Newspaper Editors," April 20, 1961, "American Society of Newspaper Editors 4/20/61" folder, Box 34, President's Office Files, Speech Files, JFKL.

38. On the White House meeting, and for a general history of the Bay of Pigs invasion, see James G. Blight and Peter Kornbluh, *Politics of Illusion: The Bay of Pigs Invasion Reexamined*, 168–69. I am grateful to Carl Kaysen, who was deputy to National Security advisor McGeorge Bundy, 1961–63, for bringing this book to my attention in an interview on his work in the White House, Cambridge, Mass., March 26, 1999.

39. Memo, McGeorge Bundy to the president, March 15, 1961, in Blight and Kornbluh, eds., *Politics of Illusion*, 220–21.

40. Memo, Arthur M. Schlesinger to the president, February 11, 1961, in Blight and Kornbluh, eds., *Politics of Illusion*, 218–19.

41. Memo, Schlesinger to the president, March 15, 1961, in Blight and Kornbluh, eds., *Politics of Illusion*, 223.

42. The typed draft reads "to our treaty obligations"; the word "treaty" has been crossed out and the somewhat more ambiguous, less legalistic word "international" has been substituted.

43. "The Nation," *Time,* April 28, 1961, 12.

44. Don Shannon, "Kennedy Tells Nation: U.S. Won't Abandon Cuba to Communists," *Los Angeles Times,* April 21, 1961, sec. 1, p. 1.

45. Holmes Alexander, "Kennedy Address to the Editors Raises Some Disturbing Questions," *Los Angeles Times,* April 27, 1961, sec. 3, p. 5.

46. Alexander, "Kennedy Address to the Editors," 5.

47. Robert Healy, "Kennedy Now Determined Castro to Go," *Boston Globe,* April 21, 1961, 1.

48. "The Nation," *Time,* April 28, 1961, 11.

49. Robert Healy, "Kennedy Draws the Line . . . the Fighting Speech," *Boston Globe,* April 21, 1961, 1.

50. "Usefulness of the Cuban Failure," *Los Angeles Times,* April 23, 1961, sec. C, p. 3.

51. John Hightower, "Kennedy's New Frontier Has Grim Awakening," *Los Angeles Times,* April 30, 1961, sec. D, p. 1.

52. "The Periscope," *Newsweek,* May 8, 1961, 21.

53. "The Periscope," *Newsweek,* May 1, 1961, 17.

54. John F. Kennedy, "The President's News Conference of April 21, 1961," *The Public Papers of the President* (1961), 312–13.

55. "Lessons to Learn," *Boston Globe,* April 22, 1961, 4.

56. Don Shannon, "Kennedy Assumes Full Blame in Cuba Fiasco," *Los Angeles Times,* April 25, 1961, sec. 1, p. 1.

57. Don Shannon, "Kennedy and Eisenhower Meet Today," *Los Angeles Times,* April 22, 1961, 1.

58. "President on Cuba: I'm Responsible," *Boston Globe,* April 25, 1961, 1.

59. "Kennedy Shoulders It All," *Boston Globe,* April 25, 1961, 10.

60. James Reston, "Kennedy Suffers a Setback," *Los Angeles Times,* April 23, 1961, sec. C., p. 1.

61. Edwin A. Lahey and David Kraslow, "Kennedy Grinned and Bore It," *Boston Globe,* April 30, 1961, 1.

62. Robert T. Hartmann, "The Editors Meet Him Again," *Los Angeles Times,* April 21, 1961, sec. 3, p. 4.

63. Robert T. Hartmann, "Cuban Fiasco Viewed as Bipartisan Blunder; But Kennedy Takes Full Responsibility for Plan Initiated Under Eisenhower," *Los Angeles Times,* April 23, 1961, 1.

64. Robert T. Hartmann, *Palace Politics: An Inside Account.*

65. Carroll Kilpatrick, "Kennedy Asks Brother, Sorensen to Help Him Out on Foreign Policy," *Washington Post,* April 27, 1961, A2. See also Richard Neustadt, *Presidential Power.*

Chapter 3

1. Memo, Megan Desnoyers to the file, January 31, 1979, Box 1, White House Staff Files, John Romagna File, President Kennedy's Speeches, JFKL.

2. Bound transcripts, President Kennedy's Speeches—1961, John Romagna, Official Reporter, Box 1, White House Staff Files, John Romagna's Files, President Kennedy's Speeches, JFKL.

3. "The President's Press Conference of January 25, 1961," *The Public Papers of the President* (1961), 10.

4. "The President's Press Conference of January 25, 1961," 14.

5. Transcript, JFK Backgrounder at State, April 25, 1961, "Presidential Backgrounder 4/25/61" folder, Box 134, White House Staff Files, Pierre Salinger, JFKL, 4.

6. JFK Backgrounder at State, April 25, 1961, 8–10.

7. Memo, Schlesinger to John F. Kennedy, April 7, 1961, "American Newspaper Publishers Association 4/22/61 Draft & Memoranda, 4/7/61—5/2/61 & Undated" folder, Box 60, Theodore C. Sorensen Papers, JFK Speech Files 1961–63, JFKL. Schlesinger sent a copy of the memo to Sorensen, with a covering note. It is the copy that is cited here.

8. Pierre Salinger, *With Kennedy,* 154–55.

9. Salinger, *With Kennedy,* 155, 158.

10. Memo, Salinger to Sorensen, April 17, 1961, "The Relations of the President and the Press, 1961 & n.d." folder, Box 11, White House Staff Files, Papers of Pierre E. G. Salinger, JFKL, 3.

11. Memo, Salinger to Sorensen, April 17, 1961, 4.

12. Memo, Salinger to Sorensen, April 17, 1961, 9–10.

13. Pierre Salinger, "Salinger Remarks before the Publicity Club of Chicago," Sheraton-Towers Hotel, Chicago, March 8, 1961; "Freedom of Information 1 of 4" folder, Box 142, White House Staff Files, Pierre Salinger, JFKL. This folder also contains a rough draft of the speech.

14. Letter, E. S. Pulliam, Jr., to Pierre Salinger, February 15, 1961, "Freedom of Information 4 of 4" folder, Box 143, White House Staff file, Pierre Salinger, JFKL.

15. Memo, Bundy to Sorensen, April 22, 1961, "American Newspaper Publishers Association 4/27/61 Draft & Memoranda, 4/7/61–5/2/61 & Undated" folder, Box 60, Theodore C. Sorensen Papers, JFK Speech Files 1961–63, JFKL.

16. Letter, Markel to Sorensen, April 24, 1961, "ANPA" folder, Box 60, Sorensen Papers, JFK Speech Files 61–63, JFKL.

17. James Reston, *Deadline: A Memoir*, 325–26.

18. Reston, *Deadline*, 122.

19. Letter, Markel to the president, April 24, 1961, "ANPA" folder, Box 60, Sorensen Papers, JFK Speech Files 61–63, JFKL.

20. Notes for speech draft, Lester Markel, April 24, 1961, "ANPA" folder, Box 60, Sorensen Papers, JFK Speech Files 61–63, JFKL.

21. John F. Kennedy, "The President and the Press," *The Public Papers of the President* (1961), 334.

22. Kennedy, "The President and the Press," 337.

23. "The President's News Conference of May 5, 1961," *The Public Papers of the President* (1961), 355–56.

24. "Information: News—and Responsibility," *Newsweek*, May 8, 1961, 24.

25. Don Shannon, "President Will Launch Political Speaking Tour," *Los Angeles Times*, April 27, 1961, 1.

26. Barry Goldwater, "The Responsibility for Cuba," *Los Angeles Times*, April 27, 1961, part 3, p. 4.

27. Robert T. Hartmann, "Kennedy and Press Self-Censorship," *Los Angeles Times*, April 30, 1961, C1.

28. Hartmann, "Kennedy and Press Self-Censorship," C6.

29. Don Shannon, "Press Leaders Support Plea of President," *Los Angeles Times*, April 28, 1961, 22.

30. Nick B. Williams, "Responsibility of the Press," *Los Angeles Times*, 30 April 30, 1961, C4.

31. Uncle Dudley, "In the National Interest," *Boston Globe*, April 29, 1961, 4.

32. James Marlow, "How Far Should Kennedy Plan for Self-Censorship Go?" *Boston Globe*, April 28, 1961, 9.

33. See folders on "Freedom of Information" in WH Staff Files, Salinger Papers, Boxes 142–43, JFKL. The publishers' luncheons appear to have run from May, 1961, to November, 1963, and intermittently thereafter.

34. See Daniel Boorstin, *The Image: A Guide to Pseudo-Events in America*.

The book was originally published in 1962 with the title, *The Image, or What Happened to the American Dream?* Boorstin's book, published during the Kennedy presidency, is an important marker of the period's anxiety about authenticity and representation.

35. John F. Kennedy, *Why England Slept*, xxiii. In his *President Kennedy: Profile of Power*, Richard Reeves notes that in Kennedy's April 20 speech to ASNE, "once again he returned to the dismal theme of *Why England Slept*, the shortcomings of democracy" (98).

36. Kennedy, *Why England Slept*, 223.

37. Ibid., 227.

38. Ibid., 228.

39. Ibid., 228–29.

40. Arthur M. Schlesinger, Jr., *A Thousand Days*, 248.

41. Schlesinger, *A Thousand Days*, 243. See also Reeves, *President Kennedy*, 101.

42. Kennedy, *Why England Slept*, xxv.

Off-the-Record Press Conference, "Backgrounder at State," April 25, 1961, State Department, Washington, D.C.

1. At this point in the document, which is at page F-6, there is a space, then a line reading only "ELK" followed by another line reading "[Continued on F-7]." The document was clearly typed in relays by different people.

2. This question appears at the top of page F-12 of the transcript. It appears that a new typist has taken up this section, as "THE PRESIDENT" now changes to "A," and what was formerly "Viet Nam" has now become "Viet-Nam." I have left the original here to remind the reader that the document clearly was preserved without having first been proofread for consistency, and as a reminder that as late as April, 1961, there did not seem a clear, official spelling of the Southeast Asian country in which the United States would soon be fighting a long and divisive war.

3. Here are inserted, on a separate line, just past the middle of page F-17, the initials VRV. On page F-18 a new typist takes up the job.

4. In the typescript, it appears that the typist has backspaced and typed over on the word "tapped" or "capped," with the letters t and c superimposed.

Bibliography

Adatto, Kiku. "Sound Bite Democracy: Network Evening News Presidential
Campaign Coverage, 1968 and 1988." Cambridge, Mass.: The Joan Shorenstein
Center on the Press, Politics, and Public Policy, John F. Kennedy School of
Government, Harvard University, 1990.

Agee, James, and Walker Evans. *Let Us Now Praise Famous Men.* Boston:
Houghton Mifflin, 1941.

Alger, Dean. "The Media, the Public, and the Development of Candidates'
Images in the 1992 Presidential Election." Cambridge, Mass.: The Joan
Shorenstein Center on the Press, Politics, and Public Policy, John F. Kennedy
School of Government, Harvard University, 1994.

Alsop, Joseph W., Jr. *Reporting Politics,* The Fourteenth Annual Memorial
Lecture Sponsored by the Twin Cities Local, American Newspaper Guild,
AFL-CIO, and the School of Journalism, University of Minnesota, Minneapo-
lis, October 17, 1960. Minneapolis, Minn.: American Newspaper Guild, 1960.

Ambrose, Stephen E. *Eisenhower: Soldier and President.* New York: Simon &
Schuster, 1990.

Anatol, Karl W., and John R. Bittner. "Kennedy on King: The Rhetoric of
Control." *Communication Quarterly* 16 (September 1968): 31–34.

Aronson, James. *The Press and the Cold War.* Indianapolis: Bobbs-Merrill, 1970.

Baker, Russell. "Decline and Fall." *New York Review of Books,* February 18, 1999,
4–6.

Ball, Moya Ann. "A Case Study of the Kennedy Administration's Decision-
Making Concerning the Diem Coup of November 1963." *Western Journal of
Communication* 54 (1990): 557–74.

Balutis, Alan P. "The Presidency and the Press: The Expanding Presidential Image." *Presidential Studies Quarterly* 7 (1977): 244–51.

Barrett, Harold. "John F. Kennedy before the Greater Houston Ministerial Association." *Communication Studies* 15 (1964): 259–66.

Benson, Thomas W. "Another Shooting in Cowtown." *Quarterly Journal of Speech* 67 (1981): 347–406.

———. "Conversation with a Ghost." *Today's Speech* 16 (November 1968): 71–81.

———. "Conversation with a Ghost: A Postscript." *Today's Speech* 22 (summer 1974): 13–15.

———. "Desktop Demos: New Communication Technologies and the Future of the Rhetorical Presidency." In *Beyond the Rhetorical Presidency,* edited by Martin J. Medhurst, 50–74. College Station: Texas A&M University Press, 1996.

———. "FDR at Gettysburg: The New Deal and the Rhetoric of Presidential Leadership." In *The Presidency and Rhetorical Leadership,* edited by Leroy G. Dorsey. College Station: Texas A&M University Press, 2002, 145–83.

———. "The First E-Mail Election: Electronic Networking and the Clinton Campaign." In *Bill Clinton on Stump, State, and Stage: The Rhetorical Road to the White House,* edited by Stephen Smith, 315–40. Fayetteville: University of Arkansas Press, 1994.

———. "Implicit Communication Theory in Campaign Coverage." In *Television Coverage of the 1980 Presidential Campaign,* edited by William C. Adams, 103–16. Norwood, N.J.: Ablex, 1983.

———. "Inaugurating Peace: Franklin D. Roosevelt's Last Speech." *Speech Monographs* 36 (1969): 138–47.

———. "Looking for the Public in the Private: American Lives, Un-American Activities." *Rhetoric and Public Affairs* 1, no. 1 (1998): 117–29.

———. "Rhetoric and Autobiography: The Case of Malcolm X." *Quarterly Journal of Speech* 60 (1974): 1–13.

———. "Rhetoric as a Way of Being." In *American Rhetoric: Context and Criticism,* edited by Thomas W. Benson. Carbondale: Southern Illinois University Press, 1989.

———. "Thinking through Film: Hollywood Remembers the Blacklist." In *Rhetoric and Community,* edited by J. Michael Hogan, 217–55. Columbia: University of South Carolina Press, 1998.

———. "'To Lend a Hand': Gerald Ford, Watergate, and the White House Speechwriters." *Rhetoric and Public Affairs* 1 (1998): 201–25.

Benson, Thomas W., and Carolyn Anderson. *Reality Fictions: The Films of Frederick Wiseman.* 2nd ed. Carbondale: Southern Illinois University Press, 2002.

Berquist, Goodwin F. "The Kennedy-Humphrey Debate." *Communication Quarterly* 8 (September 1960): 2–3.

Berry, Joseph P., Jr. *John F. Kennedy and the Media: The First Television President.* Lanham, Md.: University Press of America, 1987.

Beschloss, Michael R. *The Crisis Years: Kennedy and Khrushchev, 1960–1963.* New York: HarperCollins, 1991.

Bickers, William Patrick Michael. "Robert Kennedy and the American Press." Ph.D. diss., Ball State University, 1984.

Bingham, Worth, and Ward S. Just. "The President and the Press." *Reporter,* April 12, 1962, 18–23.

Blight, James G., and Peter Kornbluh, eds. *Politics of Illusion: The Bay of Pigs Invasion Reexamined.* Boulder, Colo.: Lynne Rienner, 1998.

Blight, James G., and David A. Welch. *On the Brink: Americans and Soviets Reexamine the Cuban Missile Crisis.* New York: Hill and Wang, 1989.

Boehm, Randolph, and R. Dale Grinder. *President Kennedy and the Press.* Frederick, Md.: University Publications of America, 1981.

Boehm, Randolph, R. Dale Grinder, Paul Kesaris, and John F. Kennedy. *A Guide to the Appointment Book of President Kennedy (1961–1963) [and] President Kennedy and the Press (1961–1963).* The Presidential Documents Series. Frederick, Md.: University Publications of America, 1982.

Boorstin, Daniel. *The Image: A Guide to Pseudo-Events in America.* New York: Harper & Row, 1964.

Bostdorff, Denise M. *The Presidency and the Rhetoric of Foreign Crisis.* Columbia: University of South Carolina Press, 1994.

Bostrom, Robert N. "'I Give You a Man'—Kennedy's Speech for Adlai Stevenson." *Communication Monographs* 35 (1968): 129–36.

Bradlee, Benjamin C. *A Good Life.* New York: Simon & Schuster, 1995.

———. *Conversations with Kennedy.* New York: Norton, 1975.

Brogan, Hugh. *Kennedy, Profiles in Power.* London and New York: Longman, 1996.

Brody, Richard A. *Assessing the President: The Media, Elite Opinion, and Public Support.* Stanford, Calif.: Stanford University Press, 1991.

Burke, Kenneth. *A Grammar of Motives.* Berkeley: University of California Press, 1969.

———. *A Rhetoric of Motives.* Berkeley: University of California Press, 1969.

Burner, David, and Thomas R. West. *The Torch Is Passed: The Kennedy Brothers and American Liberalism.* New York: Atheneum, 1984.

Campbell, Karlyn Kohrs, and Kathleen Hall Jamieson. *Deeds Done in Words: Presidential Rhetoric and the Genres of Governance.* Chicago: University of Chicago Press, 1990.

Cater, Douglass. *The Fourth Branch of Government.* Boston: Houghton Mifflin, 1959.

Caughie, John, ed. *Theories of Authorship.* London: Routledge & Kegan Paul, 1981.

Chase, Harold William, and Allen H. Lerman, eds. *Kennedy and the Press: The News Conferences.* New York: Crowell, 1965.

"Classic Conflict: The President and the Press." *Time,* December 14, 1962, 45–46.

Cogley, John. "The Presidential Image." *New Republic,* April 10, 1961, 29–31.

Collier, Peter, and David Horowitz. *The Kennedys: An American Drama.* New York: Warner Books, 1984.

Conoway, Carol B. "Framing Identity: The Press in Crown Heights." Cambridge, Mass.: Joan Shorenstein Center on the Press, Politics, and Public Policy, John F. Kennedy School of Government, Harvard University, 1996.

Corbett, Edward P. J. "Analysis of the Style of John F. Kennedy's Inaugural Address." In *Essays in Presidential Rhetoric,* edited by Theodore Windt and Beth Ingold, 95–104. Dubuque, Iowa: Kendall/Hunt, 1987.

Cornfield, Michael. "Presidential Rhetoric and the Credibility Gap." *Communication Research* 14 (1987): 462–69.

Cornwell, Elmer E., Jr. *Presidential Leadership of Public Opinion.* Bloomington: Indiana University Press, 1966.

Cramer, Richard Ben. *What It Takes: The Way to the White House.* New York: Random House, 1992.

Crawford, Kenneth. "News Management." *Newsweek,* March 11, 1963, 33.

———. "Politics of Courage." *Newsweek,* June 24, 1963, 41.

———. "We Got Rhythm." *Newsweek,* April 15, 1963, 37.

Crouse, Timothy. *The Boys on the Bus.* New York: Random House, 1973.

Curtin, Michael Joseph. "Defining the Free World: Prime-Time Documentary and the Politics of the Cold War." Ph.D. diss., University of Wisconsin, 1990.

Drew, Robert, Richard Leacock, and Donn Pennebaker. *Primary,* 1960. Motion Picture.

Drummond, Roscoe. "Mr. Kennedy's Calculated Risk." *Saturday Review,* February 11, 1961, 82–84.

Einhorn, Lois J. "The Ghosts Talk: Personal Interviews with Three Former Speechwriters." *Communication Quarterly* 36 (1988): 94–108.

Ellis, Richard J., ed. *Speaking to the People: The Rhetorical Presidency in Historical Perspective.* Amherst: University of Massachusetts Press, 1998.

Fedler, Fred, Ron Smith, and Milan D. Meeske. "*Time* and *Newsweek* Favor John F. Kennedy, Criticize Robert and Edward Kennedy." *Journalism Quarterly* 60 (1983): 489–96.

Ferrell, Robert H. *Ill-Advised: Presidential Health and Public Trust.* Columbia: University of Missouri Press, 1992.

Fields, Wayne. *Union of Words: A History of Presidential Eloquence.* New York: Free Press, 1996.

Fischer, John. *Magazine and Newspaper Journalism: A Comparison.* The Sixteenth Annual Memorial Lecture Sponsored by the Twin Cities Local, American Newspaper Guild, AFL-CIO, and the School of Journalism, University of Minnesota, Minneapolis, October 11, 1962. Minneapolis, Minn.: American Newspaper Guild, 1962.

Foley, John, Dennis A. Britton, and Eugene B. Everett, Jr., eds. *Nominating a President: The Process and the Press.* New York: Praeger, 1980.

Gelderman, Carol. *All the President's Words: The Bully Pulpit and the Creation of the Virtual Presidency.* New York: Walker, 1997.

Giglio, James N. *John F. Kennedy: A Bibliography.* Bibliographies of the Presidents of the United States, No. 34. Westport, Conn.: Greenwood Press, 1995.

———. *The Presidency of John F. Kennedy.* American Presidency Series. Lawrence: University Press of Kansas, 1991.

Gitlin, Todd. *Years of Hope, Days of Rage.* New York: Bantam, 1987.

Godden, Richard, and Richard Maidment. "Anger, Language, and Politics: John F. Kennedy and the Steel Crisis." In *Essays in Presidential Rhetoric,* edited by Theodore Windt and Beth Ingold, 105–24. Dubuque, Iowa: Kendall/Hunt, 1987.

Goffman, Erving. *The Presentation of Self in Everyday Life.* Garden City, N.Y.: Doubleday, 1959.

Golden, James L. "John F. Kennedy and the 'Ghosts.'" *Quarterly Journal of Speech* 52 (1966): 348–57.

Goldzwig, Steven R., and George N. Dionisopoulos. *"In a Perilous Hour": The Public Address of John F. Kennedy.* Westport, Conn.: Greenwood Press, 1995.

Goldzwig, Steven R., and George N. Dionisopoulous. "John F. Kennedy's Civil Rights Discourse: The Evolution from 'Principled Bystander' to Public Advocate." *Communication Monographs* 56 (1989): 179–98.

Goodwin, Doris Kearns. *The Fitzgeralds and the Kennedys.* New York: Simon & Schuster, 1987.

Goodwin, Richard N. *Remembering America: A Voice from the Sixties.* Boston: Little, Brown, 1988.

Greenstein, Fred L. *The Hidden-Hand Presidency: Eisenhower as Leader.* New York: Basic Books, 1982; Baltimore: Johns Hopkins University Press, 1994.

Grossman, Michael Baruch, and Martha Joynt Kumar. *Portraying the President: The White House and the News Media.* Baltimore: Johns Hopkins University Press, 1981.

Gustainis, Justin. "John F. Kennedy and the Green Berets: The Rhetorical Use of the Hero Myth." *Communication Studies* 40 (1989): 41–53.

Hahn, Dan F. "Ask Not What a Youngster Can Do for You: Kennedy's Inaugural Address." In *American Rhetoric: From Roosevelt to Reagan,* edited by Halford Ross Ryan, 160–67. Prospect Heights, Ill.: Waveland, 1987.

Hamilton, Nigel. *JFK: Reckless Youth.* New York: Random House, 1992.

Hargrove, Erwin C. *The President as Leader: Appealing to the Better Angels of Our Nature.* Lawrence: University Press of Kansas, 1998.

Hart, Roderick P. *The Sound of Leadership: Presidential Communication in the Modern Age.* Chicago: University of Chicago Press, 1987.

Hartmann, Robert T. *Palace Politics: An Inside Account.* New York: McGraw Hill, 1980.

Hellmann, John. *The Kennedy Obsession: The American Myth of JFK.* New York: Columbia University Press, 1997.

Henggeler, Paul R. *The Kennedy Persuasion: The Politics of Style since JFK.* Chicago: Ivan R. Dee, 1995.

Hinck, Edward A. *Enacting the Presidency: Political Argument, Presidential*

Debates and Presidential Character. Westport, Conn.: Praeger, 1993.

Hinckley, Barbara. *The Symbolic Presidency: How Presidents Portray Themselves*. New York: Routledge, 1990.

Hutchison, Earl R. "Kennedy and the Press: The First Six Months." *Journalism Quarterly* 38 (1961): 453–59.

Jamieson, Kathleen Hall. *Dirty Politics: Deception, Distraction, and Democracy*. New York: Oxford University Press, 1992.

————. *Packaging the Presidency: A History and Criticism of Presidential Campaign Advertising*. 3rd ed. New York: Oxford University Press, 1996.

Jamieson, Kathleen Hall, and Roderick P. Hart. "Assessing the Quality of Campaign Discourse—1960, 1980, 1988, and 1992." Philadelphia, Pa.: Annenberg Public Policy Center, University of Pennsylvania, 1996.

"JFK in the 'Bully Pulpit.'" *Newsweek*, June 24, 1963, 27–28.

Kalb, Marvin. *The Nixon Memo*. Chicago: University of Chicago Press, 1994.

Kaufer, David S. "The Ironist and Hypocrite as Presidential Symbols: A Nixon-Kennedy Analog." *Communication Quarterly* 27 (1979): 20–26.

Kennedy, John F. *Profiles in Courage*. New York: Harper & Row, 1964.

————. *Why England Slept*. New York: W. Funk, 1940: Westport, Conn.: Greenwood Press, 1981.

Kenny, Edward B. "Another Look at Kennedy's Inaugural Address." *Communication Quarterly* 13 (November 1965): 17–19.

Keogh, James. *President Nixon and the Press*. New York: Funk & Wagnalls, 1972.

Kern, Montague, and Marion Just. "How Voters Construct Images of Political Candidates: The Role of Political Advertising and Televised News." Cambridge, Mass.: The Joan Shorenstein Center on the Press, Politics, and Public Policy, John F. Kennedy School of Government, Harvard University, 1994.

Kern, Montague, Patricia W. Levering, and Ralph B. Levering. *The Kennedy Crises: The Press, the Presidency, and Foreign Policy*. Chapel Hill: University of North Carolina Press, 1983.

Kernell, Samuel. *Going Public: New Strategies of Presidential Leadership*. 3rd ed. Washington, D.C.: Congressional Quarterly Press, 1997.

Kerr, Harry P. "John F. Kennedy." *Quarterly Journal of Speech* 46 (1960): 241.

Kirschten, Dick. "The White House Press: Public Watchdog or Megaphone for President's Messages?" *National Journal* 17, no. 46 (1985): 2580–85.

Kluckhohn, Frank L. *America, Listen! An Up-to-the-Minute Report on the Chaos in Today's Washington. The Fumblings of the Kennedy Administration. The Search for Power. The Image Building. The Wielding of Influence on Business and the Press.* Completely updated new enl. ed. Derby, Conn.: Monarch Books, 1963.

Kornbluh, Peter, ed. *Bay of Pigs Declassified.* New York: The New Press, 1998.

Kumar, Martha Joynt, and Michael Baruch Grossman. *Images of the White House in the Media.* American Political Science Association. Proceedings, 1980.

Kurtz, Howard. *Spin Cycle.* Rev. ed. New York: Touchstone, 1998.

Kuypers, Jim A. *Presidential Crisis Rhetoric and the Press in the Post–Cold War World.* Edited by Robert E. Denton, Jr. Praeger Series in Political Communication. Westport, Conn.: Praeger, 1997.

Lang, Gladys Engel, and Kurt Lang. *The Battle for Public Opinion: The President, the Press, and the Polls during Watergate.* New York: Columbia University Press, 1983.

Lichter, Robert, and Ted Smith. "Why Elections Are Bad News: Media and Candidate Discourse in the 1996 Presidential Primaries." *Harvard International Journal of Press/Politics* 1, no. 4 (1996): 15–35.

Liebovich, Louis. *The Press and the Modern Presidency: Myths and Mindsets from Kennedy to Clinton.* Westport, Conn.: Praeger, 1998.

Lincoln, Evelyn. *My Twelve Years with John F. Kennedy.* New York: David McKay, 1965.

Ling, David A. "A Pentadic Analysis of Senator Edward Kennedy's Address to the People of Massachusetts, July 25, 1969." *Communication Studies* 21 (1970): 81–86.

Lippmann, Walter. "Managed News." *Newsweek,* April 15, 1963, 23.

Lowi, Theodore J. *The Personal President: Power Invested, Promise Unfulfilled.* Ithaca, N.Y.: Cornell University Press, 1985.

Mailer, Norman. *Miami and the Siege of Chicago.* New York: New American Library, 1968.

Maltese, John Anthony. *Spin Control: The White House Office of Communications and the Management of Presidential News.* Chapel Hill: University of North Carolina Press, 1992.

May, Ernest R., and Philip D. Zelikow, eds. *The Kennedy Tapes: Inside the White House during the Cuban Missile Crisis.* Cambridge: The Belknap Press of Harvard University Press, 1997.

Mayhew, Henry. *London Labour and the London Poor.* 1861–1862. Reprint, New York: Dover, 1968.

McClerren, Beryl F. "Southern Baptists and the Religious Issue during the Presidential Campaigns of 1928 and 1960." *Communication Studies* 18 (1967): 104–12.

McGinniss, Joe. *The Selling of the President, 1968.* New York: Trident, 1969.

Medhurst, Martin J. "Eisenhower's 'Atoms for Peace' Speech: A Case Study in the Strategic Use of Language." *Communication Monographs* 54 (1987): 204–20.

Medhurst, Martin J., ed. *Beyond the Rhetorical Presidency.* College Station: Texas A&M University Press, 1996.

Miroff, Bruce. *Pragmatic Illusions: The Presidential Politics of John F. Kennedy.* New York: David McKay, 1976.

Morris, Dick. *Behind the Oval Office.* Los Angeles: Renaissance Books, 1999.

Murphy, John M. "Comic Strategies and the American Covenant." *Communication Studies* 40 (1989): 266–79.

"The Nation." *Time,* April 28, 1961, 11–12.

"The Nation." *Time,* May 5, 1961, 14.

Nelson, W. Dale. *Who Speaks for the President? The White House Press Secretary from Cleveland to Clinton.* Syracuse, N.Y.: Syracuse University Press, 1998.

Neustadt, Richard E. *Presidential Power.* New York: Wiley, 1960.

———. *Presidential Power and the Modern Presidents: The Politics of Leadership from Roosevelt to Reagan.* Rev. ed. New York: Free Press, 1990.

Newfield, Jack. *Robert Kennedy: A Memoir.* New York: Bantam Books, 1969.

"News—and Responsibility." *Newsweek,* May 8, 1961, 24–25.

O'Donnell, Kenneth P., David F. Powers, and Joe McCarthy. *"Johnny, We Hardly Knew Ye": Memories of John Fitzgerald Kennedy.* Boston: Little, Brown, 1972.

Olson, Kathryn M. "Rhetoric and the American President." Review of Richard J. Ellis, editor. *Speaking to the People: The Rhetorical Presidency in Historical Perspective.* Amherst: University of Massachusetts Press, 1998. *The Review of Communication* 1, no. 2 (2001): 247–53.

Orwell, George. *Down and out in Paris and London.* 1933. Reprint, New York: Berkley, 1963.

Ostman, Ronald E., William A. Babcock, and J. Cecilia Fallert. "Relation of Questions and Answers in Kennedy's Press Conferences." *Journalism Quarterly* 58 (1981): 575–81.

Parmet, Herbert S. *Jack: The Struggles of John F. Kennedy.* New York: Dial, 1980.

———. *JFK: The Presidency of John F. Kennedy.* New York: Penguin, 1984.

Patterson, Thomas E. *The Mass Media Election: How Americans Choose Their President.* New York: Praeger, 1980.

———. *Out of Order.* New York: Vintage Books, 1994.

Pauley, Garth. *The Modern Presidency and Civil Rights: Rhetoric on Race from Roosevelt to Nixon.* College Station: Texas A&M University Press, 2001.

Pearce, Kimber Charles. *Rostow, Kennedy, and the Rhetoric of Foreign Aid.* East Lansing: Michigan State University Press, 2001.

"The Periscope." *Newsweek,* May 1, 1961, 17.

"The Periscope." *Newsweek,* May 8, 1961, 21.

Perrett, Geoffrey. *Jack: A Life like No Other.* New York: Random House, 2001.

Pollard, James E. "The Kennedy Administration and the Press." *Journalism Quarterly* 41 (1964): 3–14.

Pratt, James W. "An Analysis of Three Crisis Speeches." *Western Journal of Communication* 34 (1970): 194–203.

Reeves, Richard. *President Kennedy: Profile of Power.* New York: Simon & Schuster, 1993.

Reston, James. *Deadline: A Memoir.* New York: Random House, 1991.

Roberts, Charles Wesley. *The President and the Press.* Minneapolis, 1966.

Ross, Lillian. *Picture.* New York: Rinehart, 1952.

Rozell, Mark J. *In Contempt of Congress: Postwar Press Coverage on Capitol Hill.* Praeger Series in Political Communication. Westport, Conn.: Praeger, 1996.

———. "President Carter and the Press: Perspectives from White House Communications Advisers." *Political Science Quarterly* 105, no. 3 (1990): 419–34.

———. *The Press and the Bush Presidency.* Praeger Series in Presidential Studies. Westport, Conn.: Praeger, 1996.

———. *The Press and the Carter Presidency.* Boulder, Colo.: Westview Press, 1989.

———. *The Press and the Ford Presidency.* Ann Arbor: University of Michigan Press, 1992.

Salinger, Pierre. *With Kennedy.* Garden City, N.Y.: Doubleday, 1966.

Schlesinger, Arthur M., Jr. *Robert Kennedy and His Times.* New York: Ballantine, 1978.

———. *A Thousand Days: John F. Kennedy in the White House*. Boston: Houghton Mifflin, 1965.

Sharp, Harry, Jr. "Live from Washington: The Telecasting of President Kennedy's News Conferences." *Journal of Broadcasting and Electronic Media* 13 (1968): 23–32.

Silvestri, Vito N. *Becoming JFK: A Profile in Communication*. Westport, Conn.: Praeger, 2000.

Sorensen, Theodore C. *Decision-Making in the White House: The Olive Branch or the Arrows*. New York: Columbia University Press, 1963.

———. *Kennedy*. New York: Bantam, 1965.

Spragens, William C. "Kennedy Era Speech Writing, Public Relations, and Public Opinion." *Presidential Studies Quarterly* 14 (1984): 78–86.

Sweeney, Michael S. *Secrets of Victory: The Office of Censorship and the American Press and Radio in World War II*. Chapel Hill: University of North Carolina Press, 2001.

Tebbel, John, and Sarah Miles Watts. *The Press and the Presidency: From George Washington to Ronald Reagan*. New York: Oxford University Press, 1985.

Thompson, Kenneth W., ed. *The Kennedy Presidency: Portraits of American Presidents*. Lanham, Md.: University Press of America, 1985.

Tulis, Jeffrey K. *The Rhetorical Presidency*. Princeton, N.J.: Princeton University Press, 1987.

Wagner, Gerard A. "JFK and the Offshore Islands." *Communication Quarterly* 15 (April 1967): 27–29.

White, Theodore H. *The Making of the President, 1960*. New York: Atheneum, 1962.

Wills, Garry. *The Kennedy Imprisonment: A Meditation on Power*. New York: Pocket Books, 1983.

———. *Lincoln at Gettysburg: Words That Remade America*. New York: Simon & Schuster, 1992.

Windt, Theodore. "The Presidency and Speeches on International Crises: Repeating the Rhetorical Past." In *Essays in Presidential Rhetoric*, edited by Theodore Windt and Beth Ingold, 125–34. Dubuque, Iowa: Kendall/Hunt, 1987.

———. "Seeking Detente with Superpowers: John F. Kennedy at American University." In *Essays in Presidential Rhetoric*, edited by Theodore Windt and Beth Ingold, 135–48. Dubuque, Iowa: Kendall/Hunt, 1987.

Windt, Theodore, and Beth Ingold, eds. *Essays in Presidential Rhetoric.* 2nd ed. Dubuque, Iowa: Kendall/Hunt, 1987.

Windt, Theodore Otto, Jr. *Presidents and Protesters: Political Rhetoric in the 1960s.* Tuscaloosa: University of Alabama Press, 1990.

Wofford, Harris. *Of Kennedys and Kings: Making Sense of the Sixties.* New York: Farrar, Strauss, & Giroux, 1980.

Newspaper Articles

"Aide Denies Kennedy Has Suppressed News." *Los Angeles Times,* April 20, 1961, 4.

"Atty. Gen. Kennedy Asks Press Help." *Boston Globe,* April 21, 1961, 5.

"Cabinet Officers Told to Mention President." *New York Times,* April 27, 1961, A12.

"Censorship for Security." *Los Angeles Times,* April 28, 1961, sec. 1, p. 2.

"Censorship in Pentagon up, GOP Charges." *Los Angeles Times,* April 20, 1961, 4.

"Cuba Rebels Defeated, Says Castro; Kennedy Cancels Cruise." *Boston Globe,* April 20, 1961, 1.

"Depressed Areas Bill Is Passed—Kennedy Victory." *Boston Globe,* April 27, 1961, 45.

"Dr. King Praises Speech as 'a Hallmark in History'." *New York Times,* June 12, 1963, 22.

Fleeson, Doris. "Dulles May Lose CIA Job." *Boston Globe,* April 28, 1961, 16.

Folliard, Edward T. "Guard U.S. Security, Kennedy Urges Press." *Washington Post,* April 28, 1961, A1.

Fraser, Hugh Russell. "No More Jibes at the President!" *Los Angeles Times,* April 20, 1961, sec. 3, p. 5.

"Freedom and the Press." *New York Times,* April 28, 1961, A30.

Hartmann, Robert T. "Democrats Ask Kennedy News Drive: Use of All Media Urged to Support New Frontier." *Los Angeles Times,* April 28, 1961, sec. 1, p. 22.

"Havana TV Boasts 176 New Captives; Radio Slams Kennedy, Hits Cardinal Spellman." *Boston Globe,* April 25, 1961, 1.

Healy, Robert. "Kennedy May Halt All Trade with Cuba; Sees Rockefeller." *Boston Globe,* April 26, 1961, 1.

Hightower, John. "Russians Already Boastful; Feat Will Make It Harder to for Kennedy to Deal with K." *Boston Globe,* April 12, 1961, 12.

Holmes, Alexander. "The President's Fortunes Decline as Cuban Policy Meets Criticism." *Los Angeles Times,* April 24, 1961, sec. 3, p. 5.

"In Hope . . . And Agony: Kennedy Rides out His First 100 Days with Tiger by Tail." *Boston Globe,* April 29, 1961, 1.

"Kennedy Affirms Tough Stand." *Boston Globe,* April 21, 1961, 1.

"Kennedy Called Aware of Handicapped Needs." *Los Angeles Times,* April 28, 1961, sec. 1, p. 20.

"Kennedy Opens News Channels, Editors Told." *Los Angeles Times,* April 21, 1961, sec. 1, p. 4.

McGrory, Mary. "A Hot Latin and a Cool Cat." *Boston Globe,* April 26, 1961, 8.

"Mr. Kennedy, Too." *Boston Globe,* April 12, 1961, 46.

"Nation's Publishers Will Open Convention Today." *Los Angeles Times,* April 24, 1961, sec. 1, p. 6.

"No War Ever Posed So Great a Threat to U.S. as World Communism, Kennedy Tells Press." *Boston Globe,* April 28, 1961, 1.

O'Donnell, Richard. "Harvard's Cicero Had Latin Ghost Writer." *Boston Globe,* April 28, 1961, 17.

Porter, Russell. "President Urges Press Limit News That Helps Reds." *New York Times,* April 28, 1961, A1.

"President Urges Big U.S. Effort." *Boston Globe,* April 29, 1961, 1.

"The Real Issue of Survival." *Los Angeles Times,* April 21, 1961, sec. 3, p. 4.

Reston, James. "The Arts of Black Magic and the Press." *New York Times,* April 26, 1961.

"Secrecy and Security." *Washington Post,* April 29, 1961, A10.

Shain, Percy. "Ch. 4 Gives Everybody 'Piece of White House.'" *Boston Globe,* April 12, 1961, 43.

Shannon, Don. "President Urges Press to Censor News Aiding Reds." *Los Angeles Times,* April 28, 1961, 1.

———. "U.S. Is Chief Defender of Freedom: Kennedy." *Los Angeles Times,* April 29, 1961, 1.

"Text of Kennedy's Speech to Publishers." *New York Times,* April 28, 1961, A14.

"Threatening, Crackpot Letters to Kennedy Hit 2000 a Month." *Boston Globe,* April 26, 1961, 4.

Whipple, Charles L. "Aussie Rescuer Due to Meet Kennedy Again." *Boston Globe,* April 30, 1961, 58.

Wilson, Victor. "Cabinet Told to Get Plugging and Shine up Kennedy Image."
   Boston Globe, April 27, 1961, 1.

Newspapers

Boston Globe, April 12–30, 1961.
Los Angeles Times, April 20–30, 1961.
Washington Post, April 27, 1961.

Index

ISBN 1-58544-281-X